$AVE SMART, EARN MORE

THE NEW RULES FOR RETIREMENT INVESTING

DENNIS BLITZ

BUSINESS

AVON, MASSACHUSETTS

Published by Adams Business, an Imprint of
Adams Media, an F+W Publications Company
57 Littlefield Street, Avon, MA 02322. U.S.A.
www.adamsmedia.com

ISBN-10: 1-59869-645-9
ISBN-13: 978-1-59869-645-5

Printed in Canada.

J I H G F E D C B A

Library of Congress Cataloging-in-Publication Data
is available from the publisher.

This publication is designed to provide accurate and authoritative information
with regard to the subject matter covered. It is sold with the understanding
that the publisher is not engaged in rendering legal, accounting, or other
professional advice. If legal advice or other expert assistance is required, the
services of a competent professional person should be sought.
—From a *Declaration of Principles* jointly adopted by a Committee of the
American Bar Association and a Committee of Publishers and Associations

Many of the designations used by manufacturers and sellers to distinguish
their product are claimed as trademarks. Where those designations appear in
this book and Adams Media was aware of a trademark claim, the designations
have been printed with initial capital letters.

This book is available at quantity discounts for bulk purchases.
For information, please call 1-800-289-0963.

DEDICATION

Maybe the reason we write books is so we can dedicate the effort to the people who mean the most to us. As an author, you start to think about the dedication very early in the process; you want it to be right and to express your appreciation. Then the publisher calls and says it's due now. I know that this dedication will leave unmentioned many very important people, and to them I apologize.

To my parents, Mary and Lou Blitz. No matter how long we go to school, we learn all our important lessons at home.

To my four wonderful children, Marla, Lauren, Jason, Brian, plus the two more who joined our family and made it even better, Stacy and Andrew. To four fantastic and brilliant grandchildren, Carter, Sammy, Lily, and Gabe. My children and grandchildren have brought me more happiness than I could have wished for.

And, most importantly, to my best friend, helpful critic, and intellectual guide, the "Redhead from Southfield," my wife Gayle.

Dennis

CONTENTS

INTRODUCTION

This Message Could Mean an Extra Million Dollars for You and Your Family

Each year, millions of intelligent and prudent people set aside money for their future. For many, saving money is a struggle. Yet even in the face of higher costs of living and unexpected emergencies, they continue. Sadly, too often their efforts are rewarded with dreadfully poor returns.

Newspaper headlines, television talk shows, and investment company sales literature continue to proclaim that Americans need to "save more." For many, that advice is sheer nonsense. Millions of Americans are already saving and investing billions of dollars each year. The following figures represent net investment inflow for 2006.

Investment Type	Investment Amount
U.S. mutual funds	$17 trillion
Exchange-traded funds (ETFs)	$1.2 trillion
Unit investment trusts (Source: Investment Company Institute)	$29 billion
Annuity purchases (Source: LIMRA International)	$240 billion

In addition, people are investing in real estate, new businesses, and a host of other opportunities.

So, why do we keep reading that Americans are saving *less* than ever before? As the old saying goes, "Figures don't lie, but liars figure." Many of the figures we read in the headlines are derived by using an outdated measuring tool, the net inflow into bank savings accounts. However, for many of us bank savings accounts are no longer the preferred method of saving, so this indicator keeps shrinking. This obsolete indicator is frequently cited by the investment industry to make its self-serving point.

The real reason for the disappointing balances in our savings and investment accounts is that those accounts are earning abysmal returns.

The impact of even a slight improvement in our annual return will have a dramatic effect on our financial future. Let's look at an example. Joe has worked at the same company for fifteen years. The company is good to Joe and provides him with a 401(k) plan. Joe contributes to the 401(k) plan religiously (smart move, Joe). This year he will contribute $4,000, and his employer will match 50 percent ($2,000) for a total contribution of $6,000. At the beginning of the year, Joe's 401(k) account has a balance of $92,000.

Assuming that Joe invests the $6,000 on the last day of the year, take a look at how dramatically various returns impact his account balance.

Beginning Balance	Return %	Return Amount	Amount of Contribution	Ending Balance
$92,000	4.5	$4,140	$6,000	$102,140
$92,000	9.5	$8,740	$6,000	$106,740
$92,000	12.5	$11,040	$6,000	$109,040

As you can see, the *return* on Joe's investments has a greater impact on the growth of his account than the amount of his annual contribution. Over Joe's career, the impact of performance will add or subtract hundreds of thousands of dollars from his account. For those who earn or save more than Joe, the impact could be as high as $1 million over a lifetime.

Yet, rather than being advised to monitor the returns on our investments, why are we instead told that we must save more?

You need only look to the source of the "save more" mantra. For the most part, this advice comes from studies that are commissioned and distributed by the investment industry. We should view these studies with the same suspicion we reserve for studies done by drug companies—you know, the ones that always find that we should take more drugs. The investment industry benefits each time we invest more of our money. In 2006 the mutual fund industry alone collected commissions and annual investment fees of $200 billion.

The Rich Do Get Richer . . . Because They Know How to Invest

Of course, we cannot simply blame the investment industry for our poor investment returns. The fundamental barrier on our road to investment success is: most Americans have never been taught how to invest. Unfortunately, we can't look to the investment industry to teach us how to invest. Just as casinos earn the bulk of their money from inexperienced gamblers, the investment industry thrives on passive, unskilled investors. Such investors:

- Are less likely to question fees and charges.

- Are less likely to demand premium results when paying a premium fee.

- Are less skeptical of inflated sales claims.

In spite of the industry's claims that we must save more, the real path to successful investment results is to improve our annual returns.

Now, here is the good news: Achieving higher annual investment returns is not an insurmountable task. We all can earn better returns if we are willing to become a little more knowledgeable about investing.

Anyone can learn how to earn more from their investments. I know, because I have taught investment techniques to thousands of people over the years.

Why I Wrote This Book

In 1969, I graduated from college with every intention of becoming a certified public accountant. However, as I walked out the doors of the university, I decided that I wanted to first spend a little time following my passion.

What held excitement for me? Money. No, not the big stacks of money that you use to buy a red convertible. Instead, I was fascinated with the concept of money—how it moves, how it flows. I wanted to know how capital is accumulated and who ends up with it when the music stops playing.

So, instead of walking to the nearest accounting office to apply for a job, I went to the nearest stock brokerage branch and took a job in the back office. One day, as I sat at my desk, armed with a love for the market and a degree in finance and accounting, lightning struck.

Three new broker candidates had just returned from taking the test all brokers must pass before they have contact with clients, the National Association of Securities Dealers (NASD) exam. Their faces were ashen. The old exams that the branch manager had given them to study were of no value. Apparently, NASD suspected that some brokers were better at "dialing and smiling" than at understanding the rules and concepts of the market. So, NASD upgraded their entry-level exams.

Those three prospective new brokers gathered near where I sat and started asking each other about the exam. They weren't trying to figure out the right answers to the questions; they were asking what the questions meant. It was clear they knew nothing (and I mean *nothing*) about the market. That evening, I went to the branch manager. I suggested that I could write a class for new candidates on market basics. The manager was so delighted he said that he would pay me $25 to teach the class. By the next morning, however, he had changed his mind and suggested that I collect whatever I could from the new recruits. He mumbled that the recruits would be more attentive if they had their own money on the line.

It didn't matter that I might not get paid; I was off and running. I taught my first class the following week. In nine months, my little "Market Basics" class had become a three-and-a-half day "NASD Exam Prep Course," with its own textbook, fancy slides, and cool classroom handouts. Within a year, I had quit my job at the brokerage firm and was conducting classes for a half dozen branches of various brokerage firms.

Over the next fifteen years, my school grew to offer hundreds of classes annually coast to coast, and the client list read like a *Who's Who* of blue-chip financial giants. By 1985, when I sold the business, we were conducting classes for more than one of every three new security representatives in the United States and had added courses in tax shelters, insurance, and annuities.

My experience gave me a unique opportunity. Whereas most people think about investments maybe 1 percent of the time (if that much), I was in the investment world every day. I was in the product-development meetings at almost every major home office. I was not confined to any one company or any one product. I had the opportunity to consult on new investment products still in the developmental stage. I came to understand how the insurance and investment companies design products and how they make their money.

In 1989, I joined Dearborn Financial Publishing, which just a few years earlier had purchased the company that had acquired my old school. I became president of Dearborn, and in 1998 I helped sell the company to the Washington Post Organization, where it remains and continues to thrive today. Its new name is Kaplan Professional, and it is a part of the Washington Post's billion-dollar education division.

These developments gave me the time and opportunity to return to what I enjoy the most—being a full-time investor. They also motivated me to write down what I have learned. The result is *Save Smart, Earn More*.

How You Can Improve Your Investment Results

With a little knowledge, you can improve your investment returns by 20 percent, 30 percent, or more. When you finish reading this book, you will understand and be able to apply:

- The Nine Rules of Successful Investing, used by the world's most successful investors

- The critical flaw in the conventional wisdom about diversification, and how you should diversify to achieve superior profits

- The one element necessary for success in the stock market

- How to find the hidden fees you are paying for investment products and how a do-it-yourself approach can be more profitable

- How to decide when paying an investment fee is the right thing for you to do

- How to earn twelve dividend checks a year from every stock you own, even if the company is not paying a dividend

- What you need to know before investing in a franchise

- Why you—and no one else—must maintain control of your investments

This book contains no magic formulas, financial tricks, or sleights of hand. The techniques are not difficult or complex. You can handle most of the investments we talk about in this book yourself, with no need to give up control of your funds to anyone else. In fact, you will learn that many times the simplest investments are the best.

Save Smart, Earn More contains the practical and proven techniques that America's most successful investors use every day. These strategies will stick with you for the rest of your investment career. As you use what you learn in this book, you will stop jumping hopscotch-style from one investment to another, selling each as it loses money and buying the next investment at or near its top. Best of all, you will be able to stop wrestling with an investment portfolio that is just a cluster of parts and pieces, none of which fits together to move you toward your goal.

By the time you finish reading this book, your approach to investing will no longer be driven by emotional blasts of concern about being left behind. Instead, you will be able to draw upon a cohesive set of straightforward strategies that will provide you with peace of mind— and a lot of extra money, to boot. Your newfound understanding of investing will bring you the sense of control and comfort that your investments *should* provide.

If Only

Many of us can remember our parents or grandparents saying, "If I were only twenty years younger, I would have bought all the XYZ stock I could get my hands on, and today we would be rich." Or, "I'd have invested in or started that business I was thinking about, and today we would be rich." Or, "I'd have bought that piece of property where the interstate crosses the state line, and today we would be rich."

At various times in their lives, our parents and grandparents may have thought that all the good opportunities were gone. However, that has never been true. Every decade brings a new crop of opportunities from which investors have profited. Some opportunities result from transformations in the economy, but most come about from changes in the way people do everyday things:

- Americans once loved to shop at Sears, then at K Mart, then at Wal-Mart.

- They bought books first at the corner bookstore, then at mall bookstores, then Amazon.com.

- They looked up contacts in the Yellow Pages, then through Mosaic, then through Google.

- They traveled by stagecoach, then by train, by bus, and by airplane.

- They were entertained by vaudeville, then by radio, the movies, network TV, cable, and then by satellite.

The opportunities are always there. What our parents and grandparents were really lamenting was, "I'm too old to benefit from the opportunities that are available today."

Well, I have good news for everyone reading this book.

We are not too old. As a matter of fact, in "investment years" we are much younger than our grandparents were at the same chronological age. Of course it would have been a good idea to begin a brilliant investment career at the age of twenty-five. However, whether you are forty-five or sixty-five, you are likely to be around for a long time—maybe twenty years longer than just two generations ago. We have plenty of time to allow our investments to develop and mature.

Let's start our brilliant investment career today. That way, in the future, no one will have to listen to us say, "If I were only twenty years younger."

There Is a Drawback

Everyone can benefit from the techniques in *Save Smart, Earn More*, but not everyone will. To benefit from what you will learn here, you must take some action. Unfortunately, not everyone will take that step. Many people are content to simply continue checking the default boxes in their 401(k) or mutual fund investment account. For those people, *Save*

Smart, Earn More may be interesting to read, but it won't help improve their investment results.

However, if your goal is to greatly improve your investment results and you are willing to take charge of your investments to achieve that result, this book is your guide.

Every person is unique, and each of us will determine how much time we are willing to contribute to the management of our investments. Hence, I have organized this book to provide information for readers at various levels of investment activity. Part I contains the Nine Rules of Successful Investing. These are the rules that separate great investors from the rest. Part II describes how to put the nine rules into action through proven techniques for investing in stocks, options, and annuities. Readers who are willing to invest both time and money will benefit from the details presented in Part III.

The single most important point every investor must keep in mind as they invest for their future is: *Improving investment return by just a few points is more important to our results than saving more and more of our hard-earned dollars each year.*

We're ready to begin.

Part 1:

WELCOME TO THE BACK PORCH

1: We Still Have Plenty of Time to Get Rich

Don't Bother Me with the Details; Just Tell Me Where to Get My Extra Million Dollars.

Several years ago, my wife and I bought a second home near a lake in a quiet town about sixty miles from our full-time home in Chicago. The only change we made to our lake house was to add a large and comfortable enclosed porch. Most weekends we drive there on Friday afternoon and stay through Sunday. Our favorite times are when friends join us for a "weekend in the country."

In the evenings, after dinner is done, the grill has been cleaned, and the dishes put away, the evening air cools and the conversation warms. The exchange between friends takes on a familiar pattern. First is talk of family, followed by everyone's comments about politics and the latest good book or movie.

Then the conversation sometimes takes a turn that reflects a problem troubling millions of Americans: How can we best manage our finances during the time leading up to and during our retirement? At some point in the conversation, it's almost a certainty that someone will look skyward and voice one of the following:

- I just want to invest my savings to maximize return.

- I just want to invest my savings to maximize growth.

- I just want to invest my savings to maximize safety.

Some people will say all three.

As I've listened to my friends over the years, it has seemed almost as though they were waiting for divine intervention. Maybe they were hoping for a deep voice to issue forth from the heavens and intone, "Buy GE at $37 a share!" Please don't misunderstand me: The people who gather on my back porch are not uneducated or simple. These are intelligent, successful professionals, and they are not unique. They are typical of so many Americans who "only" want better returns, better growth, and more safety from their investments.

These back-porch conversations about investing start out with a great head of steam, then slowly lose momentum as my friends shake their head over how disappointed they are with their current investment results. They begin to guess at what "perfect" investments today would be sure to give them great wealth in the future. Naturally, they never arrive at a conclusion, and the conversation eventually tails off, only to be replaced by a different topic.

But tonight, as we gather on the back porch, I suggest that we do something different.

After thirty years of writing for and lecturing to professionals on the topic of investing, I volunteer to lead a discussion on the proven rules of successful investing. Tonight, our sole focus will be on the topic of how to best manage our money for the future. I have assembled on my porch some of the smartest people I know, and I want you to join us.

Tonight, we will all ignore any past investment screw-ups that we may have made. We will forget, for the next few hours, that maybe our current investment portfolio is a disorderly mess that has provided disappointing results. Tonight, we will all be brilliant. Our thinking on the topic of how to best manage our money will be crisp and intelligent. We will come to conclusions that will be both elegant and usable. We will do all this before the sun comes up in the morning, before we can hear the golfers' carts humming past the cottage on their way to their morning game.

As everyone gathers, I run off to the kitchen to get a fresh cup of coffee. Maybe I can find a little slice of the pie that was left from dessert. I tell the others that if pie and coffee don't interest them, there are soft drinks and something a bit stronger in the bar. Get what you like, and let's begin.

The Fundamentals of Sound Investment

As my friends return to the porch, I notice that, in addition to fresh drinks and seconds on dessert, a few have come back prepared to take notes. Even in this casual setting, people are serious when it comes to retirement savings. I suggest that we start the evening's discussion by agreeing on a few basic concepts—ideas that are fundamental to any successful approach to investment.

Concept One: This Is Important Now

Investing is no longer the icing on our future plans; instead, it's now the cake. I ask my friends if they've ever had thoughts such as these:

- "My investments today will not be adequate for me to live in the style that I hope for when I retire."

- "As my income from work decreases in the future, I will need to rely more and more on my investments to pay for the things that I want for myself and my family."

Carol laughs. "Boy, I think those thoughts all the time."

Tim interrupts and says, "Not me; I only think about them when I'm awake."

"Okay," I say, as I raise my coffee cup in a toast. "Then you already understand that your investment portfolio performance will dictate your future lifestyle. But not to worry! Even if your current investments have generated disappointing results, a fix is not out of reach. You simply need to understand the Nine Rules used by successful investors."

Lou, with tongue in cheek, asks, "Is there a successful investors' clubhouse? Will I need to discover a secret handshake or password?"

"No," I respond, "the secrets are all around us. In fact, I'll share them with you tonight. But for now, let's stick with the groundwork."

Concept Two: You Are Your Own Best Investment Advisor

You are the one who must control how your money is invested. Although the need for intelligent investing advice has never been greater, there is a surprising lack of *unbiased* guidance for the average investor. Of course, people in the highest 5 percent of net worth have access to excellent investment advisors. The rest of us, however, must be our own best resource.

Concept Three: There Are Two Ways to Invest in Any Asset

The investment can be "do-it-yourself," which will save you substantial fees and costs but requires some knowledge, as well as an investment of your time. Or you may choose to use a professional who will charge you fees for his management services. Although it may seem the easier choice, if you are paying heavy management fees for others to make all your investments in real estate, equities, retirement planning, and small businesses, it's unlikely you'll achieve your investment goals.

Concept Four: Life Expectancy Is a Critical Part of Investment Planning

Wouldn't it be much easier if we knew exactly how long we needed to depend on our investment income? Wouldn't knowing our exact life expectancy be helpful when deciding between long-term and short-term options for our investments? Well, life doesn't operate on a set timetable, so we must depend on history to build a framework for planning our retirement finances.

According to the National Center on Health Statistics, in the year 2007, the average life span for Americans was 77.9 years. That's a helpful place to start when trying to project our future, but it's important to remember that everyone is unique. If any of the following is true about you, you are statistically likely to live longer than the average American:

- You have had generally good access to health care.

- You went to college.

- You are married or have a pet. (Some think that a pet is easier on your health than a spouse, but that's a different book.)

- Your parents are still alive (or lived to a ripe old age).

- You are not morbidly obese.

- You remain mentally active.

- You don't smoke.

As we can see, simple factors can make a difference in life expectancy. Even things as basic as a positive attitude or a sense of humor have been shown to increase longevity. The longer we live, the more money we'll need to finance our retirement—and the more time we have to make sound, long-term investment decisions. Hence, if you're a healthy, middle-aged American, you don't need to make quickie, bet-the-farm investments.

I look to my left at Mark, who has been taking notes. "What do we have so far?" I ask. As usual, Mark is to the point:

1. This is important now.

2. You can be your own best investment advisor.

3. There are two ways to invest in any asset (self-manage or pay a management fee).

4. We have plenty of time for our investments to mature.

"I agree with everything you say," says Tim. "So, why don't I feel rich?"

Eliminating Obstacles to Success

The room chuckles at Tim's exaggerated misery, but I don't want to dismiss his remark too quickly. He brings up an interesting question.

"Tim, there are five very specific obstacles that keep many people from being as successful as they would like with their investments. Once we can identify and understand those obstacles, we will be better able to avoid them."

Lou leans forward. "If there are five obstacles, I'm sure that I've bumped into every one of them without even knowing it. What are they?"

"All right," I say, laughing. "Here goes."

Obstacle Number One: Believing the Half-Truth of Mutual Fund Diversification

Every mutual fund brochure loudly proclaims that we must diversify, diversify, diversify. You've heard it a million times. The implication, of course, is that "diversification equals safety" and that no poor sap of an investor can diversify his or her portfolio as competently as a mutual fund can diversify its holdings. Mutual funds emphasize this last point by proudly proclaiming that they are invested in 300, 400, or 500 different companies. "Can you do that?" asks the salesperson, letting you know that you're Mr. Small Time compared to his company's giant investing machine.

Millions of people have bought into the mutual funds' diversification pitch. (In fact, I'll bet that most of us have.) However, if diversification equals safety, why did millions of mutual fund investors lose billions of dollars in 2000 and 2001?

The answer reveals that the mutual fund industry is telling a half-truth about its "diversity." Yes, if you invest in a mutual fund, your money is spread over hundreds of stocks. In the end, however, you still are invested in stocks and only stocks. That doesn't represent much diversity, does it?

If you want to have a diversified investment portfolio, you need to consider a broad range of investments. Let's look at a successful long-term investment program as a guide.

Harvard University's endowment portfolio is an eye-popping $27 billion. The Harvard Investment Fund buys stocks with that money, just as you do. However, only 15 percent of its assets are invested in traditional listed securities. The balance is diversified among commodities, private equity, hedge funds, bonds, foreign securities, real estate, and so on. The endowment fund has averaged a 15.9 percent return during the past ten years. At this rate the endowment fund's assets doubled every 4.5 years not counting new contributions made by Harvard's generous alumni.

Now, it's unlikely that you have $27 billion to invest or a staff of in-house investment managers to help you locate investment opportunities and monitor their performance. Still, the Harvard University endowment portfolio offers a significant lesson: You need to expand your thinking about where you place your funds. To put it bluntly, the search for diversified investment opportunities doesn't end with the list of the 500 largest companies in America. It only starts there.

Obstacle Number Two: Asking the Wrong Question about the Right Investment

I don't care if you chair an investment seminar, or appear on a television panel, the first question that you will be asked as you leave the stage will be: "What's the best place for me to put my money?" Maybe you've asked this question yourself. Sadly, it's the wrong question. Consider this scenario.

Let's assume that the person asking the question has the goal of earning the highest return possible on their investment. In that case, the answer to the question is simple: *Take all your money and buy lottery tickets.* If you select the right numbers, your return percentage will be in the millions. (Try to match that kind of return with your Vanguard mutual fund.) Of course, there is a flaw in the lottery-ticket investment strategy—the odds of winning are about 170 million to 1.

The right question, therefore, is not "What is the best *place* to invest" but "What is the best *way* to invest?" Once we learn *how* to invest, everything else will fall into place.

Obstacle Number Three: Searching for (and Expecting to Find) Unbiased Guidance

Wouldn't it be nice if there were a wise guru sitting in an unpretentious office near our home? He or she would listen endlessly to our goals, desires, hopes, and plans, then give us an unbiased and detailed road map to follow to maximize our investment returns and minimize financial frustration. There are four reasons why that person just doesn't exist:

1. Securities brokers (who are sometimes referred to as financial advisors, financial consultants, or financial planning specialists) are licensed to be a "registered representative" of a single broker/dealer. Unless they are given expressed written permission to sell outside products (a relatively rare practice known as selling away), they may only offer the products of the single broker/dealer for whom they work. This requirement was put in place to help create a clear chain of responsibility that can be used to monitor the behavior of unscrupulous brokers. However, it also limits the investment products that the broker may offer.

2. Everyone has limits. No single adviser, salesperson, or guru could understand the fine points of every investment category. The real estate expert may be at a loss to explain the ins and outs of an equity-indexed annuity, just as the annuity salesperson would be of little help in evaluating a real estate development project. *Beware*

of the investment salesperson who says, *"I specialize in all investments"*

3. The representative you speak with is likely paid by commission. There's nothing wrong with commissions, but we need to be aware that the commission might be driving the advice we receive. It's nearly impossible for a commissioned sales representative to be totally unbiased.

4. The fourth—and perhaps biggest—reason why we shouldn't rely on anyone for unbiased investment guidance is this: No one cares about our money as much as we do.

The investment of our dollars and the monitoring of their progress is up to us, and it should be—it's our money.

Obstacle Number Four: Underestimating Risk

Everyone has heard the phrase "Risk equals reward." But, I suggest that a more accurate expression of reality would be "Risk equals risk." Risk is real—write that in stone. Things sometimes go wrong:

- You buy stock in a large successful drug company. Shortly after, one of the company's new drugs is found to cause sudden cardiac arrest in people who are allergic to soy products.

- You buy investment real estate in a nice town just before the town's largest employer moves its production to China.

- You invest in a charter bus company with a book full of guaranteed business at a guaranteed fare, and gasoline prices go through the roof.

Risk is real.

Obstacle Number Five: Battling the Headwind of Management Fees

Every investor knows that there are costs associated with making and maintaining an investment. The sales literature, the salesperson who is speaking with you, the company's home-office building located in the central business district—all this costs money, and that money comes from the fees built into every investment product. The question we must keep asking is whether the fees are reasonable when compared to the service provided. To answer that question, we first must know what the fees are.

Management fees sometimes disappear into the fabric of investment presentations. Watching an investment promoter run through a fee disclosure is akin to watching a David Copperfield performance (at least Copperfield admits that he's using misdirection to keep our eye looking the other way). Too often, investors are encouraged to look at the icing while an investment promoter carries off the cake in the form of hidden fees.

Every Guarantee Has a Cost

Here is a simple question you can ask during any investment presentation. Each time the salesperson tells you about a "guarantee" offered by the product, ask about its cost. All guarantees, come at a cost:

- Guarantee of no loss: The company may reduce your upside potential to cover its risk. This can be done by capping the investor's potential growth in a rising market, by deducting an insurance premium from the funds you have invested or a combination of both.

- Guarantee of fast liquidity: To accomplish this the company will simply hold back investment funds. That is, it keeps a cash reserve to make sure it can meet redemption requests. However, being less than 100 percent invested will cause a reduction in investment efficiency.

- Guarantee of no sales fee: Check the mutual fund prospectus for a paragraph titled 12-B-1. Most no-load funds (mutual funds that do not charge a sales fee upon investment) levy 12-B-1 sales fees against your portfolio. Also look for a surrender charge (a fee charged by some funds when investors liquidate all or part of their shares) and ongoing management fees.

Does an annuity guarantee a monthly payment for the rest of your life, no matter how long you live? That guarantee comes at a cost. Does the insurance company say that if you become disabled, it will waive your premium? That guarantee, too, comes at a cost. Sometimes the cost of the guarantee is not listed in the prospectus; it is instead concealed in the form of a reduction in the upside potential of our investment dollars. The cost of each guarantee equates to a lower return, which is one of the reasons that the simplest products can in many cases provide the best returns. Ask yourself whether you really need each guarantee being offered.

We need to remain vigilant, as some salespeople like to present the most elaborate products their company offers because these products frequently pay the highest commission. If the salesperson cannot fully explain all the fees and costs of an investment to your satisfaction, it's time to look elsewhere. Only work with a salesperson who is knowledgeable about his or her product and who provides you with full disclosure of the positives *and the drawbacks of the product.*

Knowing All the Fees, All the Time

Perhaps the prospectus lists the investment management fee as a dollar amount or percentage, and the fee sounds reasonable, even low. You assume that the fee covers the cost of managing and maintaining the investment, along with the operating costs of the Mutual Fund such as accounting, legal, printing and postage, and so on. Elsewhere in the prospectus, however, you learn that operating costs are charged as a separate fee to the investors (called the expense ratio). In other words, the management fee goes straight to the management company, and the investors are left to pay all the operating costs of the fund.

Of course there are times when, even a high fee may be reasonable, especially when the work being done on your behalf by the promoter is something that you could not do yourself. The fees of a real estate limited partnership are a good example. Sure, the general partner charges for their services, but it's possible that the experience and skills the general partner brings to the project would cost you twice as much in the open market.

Lou places both hands on the top of his head. "Yep, just as I expected. I have bumped into every one of the five obstacles."

I again turn to Mark and say, "Let's recap our obstacles to investment success."

Never missing a beat, Mark reads from his notes:

- Believing the half-truth of mutual fund diversification

- Worrying about where to invest, rather than how to invest

- Expecting to find unbiased guidance, when in fact we are our own best investment manager

- Underestimating the very real risks involved in any investment

- Paying high fees

Fortunately, as we will see, there are ways to overcome each of these obstacles.

2: The First Rules of Successful Investing

When I was young I knew that I wanted to be somebody. Now I realize that I should have been more specific.

—Lily Tomlin

Bob stands, adjusting his slacks as he attempts to hide the fact that he has just let out his belt a notch. "Dinner was great, but I ate too much. Next Monday, I'm going to start going to Weight Watchers meetings."

Mark reminds everyone that about once a month for the past ten years Bob has been announcing that he is going to start Weight Watchers on the following Monday. "One of these times he may really do it," says Mark.

Bob doesn't laugh but instead dives back into the topic at hand. "We have set a foundation for investing and listed the obstacles to investment success. Are we ready to begin to identify those Nine Rules of Successful Investing?

"We are," I answer. "As we go over the nine rules, I'd like you to consider this: *Successful investors make their decisions differently from average investors.* As you understand and start to follow the rules we're about to discuss, you will be learning to think like a successful investor."

Rule One: Invest in What You Know

Successful investors know what they don't know. Not every investment is the right opportunity for every investor.

It may sound simplistic, but the first step to knowing where to invest your money is to understand where *not* to invest your money. Simply stated, you should never invest in anything you do not understand. A simple tool is the "neighbor" test; if you cannot explain an investment opportunity in clear terms to your next-door neighbor, maybe you should look for a different investment.

The poor guy who cannot identify what he will *not* invest in is a sitting duck for every hot stock tip or half-baked concept that comes along. Depending on the sales presentation and his available funds, at any given moment he may buy stocks, commodity futures, a stake in a cattle breeding ranch, a franchise, equity options, an oil well, or a real estate development project.

Now hear this! Successful investors don't think that way. Successful investors only place their funds in a few areas. Furthermore, they only place their money in areas that they clearly understand.

Standing near the bar and pouring a soft drink, Carol interrupts me. "That's interesting. I've spent my entire career working in the administrative office of both commodity exchanges in Chicago, and I know that you're right—the most successful traders only trade a few things. Some trade the grain-market commodities such as wheat, corn, and oats. Others stick with the metal markets, trading copper, gold, or silver. But you can bet that the most successful grain traders very rarely trade the metal markets, and vice versa."

Mark is quick to agree. "I've worked as a consultant with several private equity companies in the past few years," he says, "and I can tell you that the most successful ones have two characteristics. First, their offices are never glitzy or extravagant. The fancier the office space, the less money seems to be left to distribute to investors.

"The second trait is that they work in a specific or narrow category of business. The most successful private equity firms are focused on industries that they know and understand. Every now and then, a private equity firm will call me and say, 'We're looking for some place good to put our money.' I smile and agree to keep my eyes open for them, but under my breath I'm saying, 'Buddy, you can kiss your money good-bye—you're doomed before you start.' The successful firms stick with their areas of expertise."

Rule Two: Invest, Succeed, Repeat

When the successful investor finds something that works, they keep repeating the process. Simple as Rule Two sounds, too many investors treat a success as if it were just a lucky break and do not take the time to examine what they can repeat from the experience. As the nine rules keep pointing out, the method that you use to invest is much more important than what you invest in.

Countless studies have attempted to determine why some investors succeed and others do not. These studies come to the same conclusion. The way we invest is more important to our success than what we invest in. Depending on the study, the way an investor invests can have a long-term impact seven to ten times greater than what he invests in.

"Teacher, teacher," calls out Jack, waving his hand above his head, schoolboy style. "I'm not getting this." Everyone snickers. However, it's easy to understand Jack's frustration. For our whole investing career, we have been trying to figure out the best place for our investment dollars. Now we are learning that it is not "what" but "how" we invest our dollars.

"Jack," I reply, "consider this. We know that some investors do very well in the stock market; however, the majority of people struggle and are rewarded with only second-rate results. What causes this difference? The successful stock market investors are those people who have identified a profitable method of stock selection and repeat that method over and over again."

Later we will focus on stock market investing and identify the different methods of stock selection that successful investors use. Each method has the potential to make you very successful. What *doesn't* work? Not knowing your method. The person who fills his portfolio with stocks with no rhyme or reason behind their selections is condemned to a life of investment mediocrity.

Rule Three: Embrace the Learning Curve

Sticking with an investment during the learning period is not easy. Many investments are complicated and take time to learn and understand. During the learning period, we can all become disheartened. But the learning curve is part of the tuition we must pay to succeed.

Most successful investors will tell you, "When I started out, I made a lot of mistakes. I considered quitting several times. But eventually I got the hang of how the market works, and since then I've done pretty well." The most successful investors may add, "Sure, I still make mistakes and have a loss every now and then. The way I invest isn't perfect, but I've gotten a feel for investing this way, and I stick with it."

When starting out in any investment category, you *will* make mistakes. Mistakes are to be expected; don't be discouraged.

For some investors, the frustration can overrule good investment practices. If they suffer a setback in the stock market and become impatient, they may sell all of their stock and move their money into real estate. Then, after incurring a few real estate disappointments, they reverse the process and move back to stocks. People who manage their investments this way accomplish three things:

1. They are probably selling their current investments at the bottom and buying the new investment near the top.

2. They keep walking away from everything they have already learned and replacing it with a new learning curve.

3. They incur unnecessary liquidation and reinvestment costs.

"Hold on a minute," says Jack. This time he is much more intense than he was earlier. "Are you saying that the only way to be successful is to *know everything about every type of investment?*"

"Not at all," I say. "That would be impossible—and it's unnecessary. To be a really successful investor you need to develop a working knowledge in only a small area of investing, a subcategory, and stick with it. The simple truth is this: The more experience and knowledge you gain in the narrow area in which you invest, the more consistent will be your profits. Again, 'Embrace the learning curve.'"

Let's use investing in real estate as an example. It is unlikely that anyone could be expert in all forms of real estate investing. The buy-and-hold real estate investor requires different skills from someone who uses a "buy, fix, and flip" approach. People who develop raw land need to understand different rules and regulations than do the people who redevelop existing properties. Residential development requires different skills from commercial development. The most successful real estate investors stay in their subcategory and invest the time necessary to develop their knowledge and become proficient.

Select a narrow topic, take the time to learn its nuances, and you will be squarely on the path to outperforming market averages. Why?

Because most investors flit from one investment to another. The longer you stay in your area, the more likely you are to be playing against an ever-revolving pool of rookies.

Imagine a table in a Las Vegas poker room. Sitting around the table are five or six regulars. A weekend tourist on his first trip to Nevada shows up and claims the open seat. His plastic name badge says "Hello! My Name Is Ray" and "First Annual Dog and Cat Lovers Expo." Who is more likely to walk away from this table a winner, one of the regulars or Ray? The answer is clear. With an inferior knowledge of the game and a table full of experienced gamblers to play against, Ray is out of his league and on his way to the cleaners.

Investors who find success through repeated experience continue to develop their knowledge and skill in their subcategory of investing. They accept the learning curve as part of the process of developing sound investment skills.

"All right, Mark," I say, as I lean back in my chair, "let's recap the first three rules used by successful investors."

"Sure thing," he replies:

- Rule One: Rich and successful investors know what they don't know.

- Rule Two: When they identify an action that is profitable, they repeat that action again and again.

- Rule Three: Rich and successful investors understand that there is a learning curve.

As if on a cue, several people get up and walk to the coffeepot to freshen their cup. Lou is looking in the refrigerator for a bottle of ginger ale, while Jack and Tim each find something a little stronger to drink.

Anne is the first one back, looking at her notes, then at me.

"So far," she says, "the things that we have talked about are all smart rules that we should follow. However, I don't see any ideas here that I think will make us rich."

"You're right, Anne," I say. "No single idea or rule will make you rich. But when you view the Nine Rules of Successful Investing as a whole, I know you'll see their value. The next rule," I add, "is too often overlooked, yet it is the bedrock of success."

3: The Absence of Failure

As a result of my investments, I have all the money I will ever need. That is, if I die by 4:00 this afternoon.

—Henny Youngman

Just about everyone has returned to the porch. I start talking again. "Remember earlier this evening I said that underestimating risk is one of the greatest obstacles to investment success? The fourth rule of successful investing addresses exactly that point."

Successful investors know that a great part of success is simply the absence of failure. Sadly, not every investor understands this seemingly obvious point. Unlike the average investor, who typically asks first, "How much return can I earn from this investment?" the experienced, successful investor asks, "How much risk am I taking?" Sure, successful investors care about rate of return and the potential upside reward of an investment, but they care even more about the risk of loss caused by a failed investment.

Rule Four: Avoid Losing Money (Wow! What a Concept!)

Tim starts to shift his weight uncomfortably. "Wait a minute," he says. "The rich already have money, so they can afford not to reach for the stars with their investments. I need to build up wealth; once I have a big pile of money, I'll be as careful as the best of 'em."

From the corner of the room, Jack breaks in. "Hold on, Tim. The idea of considering the magnitude of *risk* before getting excited about a potential *return* makes sense. Isn't it defense that wins games? Look at the scores during the NBA finals. They are always lower than during the regular season. And don't forget NFL playoffs. The stories in the paper leading up to every playoff game are always about how one team will need to contain the other team's best receiver or running back. How can you argue with the concept that thinking defensively makes sense?"

"Sure," replies Tim, "but isn't the idea of thinking about risk before thinking about return just plain backward?"

This time Bob chimes in. "That's the way it is. If you want to drill a deep oil well, you first build a tall derrick. If you want to build a tall building, first you dig a deep footing. It may feel as though you are headed in the wrong direction, but it's the foundations that must come first."

"I have the sense that Tim is not alone in his skepticism," I say. "So let's put a pencil to this."

Most investors would be very happy with an annual return of 12 percent or 14 percent. However, many of those same people make investments that put 50 percent, 70 percent, or even 100 percent of their funds at risk. Let's look at an example using four investors. The investors each start with $100,000, and they each invest for twelve years, as follows:

- Investor One earns a steady 12.5 percent each year.

- Investor Two earns 12.5 percent each year, except for a one-time 20 percent portfolio loss in year three.

- Investor Three earns 12.5 percent each year, except for a one-time 40 percent portfolio loss in year three.

- Investor Four earns 12.5 percent each year, except for a one-time 60 percent portfolio loss in year three.

Remember these are just *one-time* losses in an otherwise good program. Twelve years after the original $100,000 investment, the impact of the losses is stunning:

- Investor One has an ending balance of $410,989.

- Investor Two has an ending balance of $292,256.

- Investor Three has an ending balance of $219,192.

- Investor Four has an ending balance of $147,030.

Every investor has to decide just how much risk he or she can tolerate. Keep in mind that following a 100 percent loss, no amount of 12.5 percent profits can ever restore an investment account to break-even status.

Bob again breaks in to the conversation. "I understand that risk is bad. However, we must take some risk, so how do we determine our limitations?"

"I'll give you a simple process for thinking about your tolerance for risk," I say. "But first let me tell you how *not* to do it."

Determining Your Personal Risk Tolerance

The "new account" form at every brokerage firm asks the question, "What is your risk tolerance?" Alternately, it might ask you to check a box that best describes your investment style, with choices ranging from Very Aggressive to Very Conservative. In reality, few people can accurately answer such a complex question with just a single check mark.

As this may be a new account, the investor is likely to be optimistic about his or her prospects and too often checks the box marked "Very Aggressive." But how often do you think the new customer would choose that option if, instead of "Very Aggressive," it read "I am willing to risk everything"?

Here is a quick exercise to help quantify your risk tolerance.

First, determine the value of your investment portfolio. I generally do not include autos, personal furnishings, or family jewelry in this list. If you sold your car tomorrow, you would need to replace it with another, and your personal furnishings and family jewelry are unlikely to be turned into cash. Include the value of any investment assets you have, such as investments in the following.

Cash and savings	Bank CDs	IRA account(s)
Stocks	Bonds	Mutual funds
Money market	Annuities	Cash value insurance
401(k)	Home equity	Vacation-home equity
Limited partnerships	Collectibles	Business interests
Real estate investments		

On a clean sheet of paper, draw a table like the one following. At the top of the "Total Portfolio" column, replace the $75,000 given in the example with the value you've just determined of your investment portfolio. To complete the second column, use your total portfolio value times the percentages in Column 1 to determine the amount of loss you would sustain at that rate in a single year. In the example Column 2 shows loss amounts assuming a total portfolio value of $75,000.

Personal Risk Tolerance Calculator for a $75,000 Portfolio

Column 1	Column 2	Column 3
Percent of one year's loss	Amount of one year loss	Personal risk tolerance ranking
5%	$3,750	
10%	$7,500	
15%	$11,250	
20%	$15,000	
25%	$18,750	
30%	$22,500	
35%	$26,250	
40%	$30,000	
45%	$33,750	
50%	$37,500	
55%	$41,250	
60%	$45,000	
65%	$48,750	
70%	$52,500	
75%	$56,250	
80%	$60,000	
85%	$63,750	
90%	$67,500	
95%	$71,250	
100%	$75,000	

Next, calculate your personal risk values.

In the third column, consider each amount of loss and ask yourself the following question: "If I lose this amount of my assets in one year . . ." Rate your response with the number that applies to the appropriate response for you:

1. This amount of loss would not be a problem.

2. This amount of loss would be somewhat easy to replace.

3. This amount of loss would be somewhat difficult to replace

4. This amount of loss would be very difficult to replace.

5. Oh my God, what have I done?

Your willingness to tolerate a percentage level of potential loss will differ from that of the next person. This is because of differences in your time horizon, your present earnings, your other financial obligations, and so on. As you look down the list, take a moment to consider just where you wanted to stop accepting risk. For many people, a "2" may represent unacceptable risk. Others will stop when they reach a "3." Few should ever accept a risk of "4" or higher.

Using Risk Tolerance Information When You Build Your Portfolio

The lower your risk tolerance level, the more you will navigate the bulk of your portfolio toward conservative investments. But, that does not mean that you cannot take some risks.

As you will learn, you should view your portfolio as a whole. Even if you are very conservative and comfortable with no more than a 5 percent risk, you will see that you can still make speculative investments. For example, if you have a $75,000 portfolio and you invested $71,250 (95 percent) in low-risk investments you are still able to make a highly speculative investment with $3,750 (5 percent). Understanding risk does not mean that you never take a risk, it means that you only accept calculated risks.

Every day people make investments in which they have examined the potential for return without giving that same level of consideration to the risk they are accepting. Some get away with that mistake, but many do not. People who ignore this fourth rule of successful investing may find themselves in the awful position of holding investments that make them poorer instead of richer.

I look around the room and can tell that everyone wants to move to the next rule. However, I want keep the focus on this topic of risk just a little longer.

The Theory of "True Zero": How to Measure Your Return When You Take a Risk

Earlier today, the kids were playing on the porch. They left behind a chalkboard. I walk to the board and proudly write "Blitz's Theory of True Zero." (I always wanted to have a theory named for me.) Even though my friends laugh (and groan), they are ready to take notes. So I begin.

The theory of True Zero refines a concept known as risk premium. Earlier, I suggested that some investment sales presentations have turned the phrase "Risk equals reward" from a warning into a sales tool. These salespeople imply that you must accept risk if you ever hope to earn a return. By using True Zero you will be able to better determine if the reward (the rate of return) you are offered is worth the risk that you are accepting.

"Let's create a baseline for our thinking," I suggest, "What if there was an investment that met each of the following criteria:

- Risk free
- Could be bought without commissions or fees
- Charged no management fee
- Required virtually none of your time to manage
- Very liquid

If such an investment existed, we could use that as our baseline when trying to measure the risk premium offered by another investment.

I look up and notice that half the people on the porch are smiling because they have already figured out where I am headed. The others are not quite sure.

"There is just such an investment," I say. "T-bills, the short-term debt issued by the federal government. T-bills have every one of the five characteristics I just listed. Hence, the current rate of return on a T-bill becomes our True Zero point. The T-bill rate is listed every day in newspapers and on Web sites and we will measure all investment returns from this baseline return, not from absolute zero (Absolute zero is that round number between -1 and +1).

Here's an example of how you can use the theory of True Zero to calculate the true risk-adjusted return of an investment.

Let's say T-bills are paying a return of 4 percent. An investment or savings opportunity comes your way that offers 6.25 percent. The opportunity also requires that you pay a 1 percent management fee, and the investment has a slim possibility of loss.

The true risk-to-reward comparison is your earnings as compared to True Zero. To find this, you subtract both the management fee and the T-bill rate from the return offered by the investment. In this example, the adjusted return is 1.25 percent (6.25 percent minus 1 percent management fee equals 5.25 percent, minus the risk-free T-bill rate of 4 percent equals 1.25 percent). If T-bill rates were higher, the adjusted return would be even less.

Remember, when describing the potential return of this investment, the salesperson and the sales literature will show the 6.25 percent figure. To have a true understanding of the risks and reward, however, you must take that one extra step that the salesperson won't take for you and compare the potential return to the risk-free rate of return available to you from T-bills. The difference between the potential return of an investment and the current T-bill rate is your reward for taking the following risks:

- Illiquidity

- Investment of your time

- Potential of failure and the loss of your capital

Hence, your question can now be "Is it worth it to me to accept the three risks listed above in order to earn a return of 1.25 percent?" Each investor will answer that question based on his or her individual situation. The lock that an understanding of True Zero opens is that we now have a more accurate measurement tool to help us decide which investments are worthwhile.

Knowing the current return on risk-free money is the starting point for making any investment decision.

At this point, I glance toward Tim, he looks like the kid who got a lump of coal for Christmas. "I am still looking to make some money, and you are suggesting that no investment beyond T-bills is worth the risk," he says.

"No, Tim," I say, "that's not my point at all. For example, for the past seventy years, the stock market has had an average increase in value of between 10 percent and 11 percent per year. During that same period, T-bills have had an average return of about 3 percent. That means there has been a very healthy 7 percent to 8 percent spread for accepting the risk. A difference of 7 to 8 percent is tremendous over a long period. The point we are making is that no investment should be made without first considering the risk-free alternative."

Carol stands up and walks around to lean on the back of her chair. "Okay," she says, laughing. "We get it. It's not that all risk is bad; we just need to know how to view risk in its proper perspective."

"And don't forget Rule Four, 'Avoid Losing Money,'" adds Mark. "We have to try to keep our investments moving forward on an even keel so we don't need to recover from big losses."

I wipe the chalkboard clean with a flourish and return to my seat. "Yep, keeping things level and balanced is very important to our long-term success.

Tim, who is now beside himself with frustration, says, "Okay, I understand that we must be careful not to take risks that will cause us to fall behind. But I still don't see how we are going to get ahead."

"Tim," I reply, as I settle back in my chair, "that brings us to the next of our nine rules."

4: The Rule of Complementary Investing

The Golden Rule of the Most Successful Investors

The sun set almost an hour ago, and Anne asks if we have an extra sweater or a light jacket. Jack freshens his coffee, and I read aloud from a list that Mark has just handed me. It gives the first four rules of successful investing:

1. Successful investors know what they don't know.

2. Successful investors identify an action that is profitable and then repeat that action again and again.

3. Successful investors understand that investing requires a learning curve.

4. Successful investors consider risk before return.

Jack looks up from his coffee and says, "Not too exciting, is it."

"I disagree," I say. What if every investor followed the four simple rules we have been talking about? What if we all simply stuck with a method of investing long enough to fully understand it? What if we had been more vigilant about risk? Wouldn't we all be much further ahead today?

I ask a question of the room.

"Who here would be wealthier if they had invested using just the four simple rules that we have already spoken about?" Everyone nods in the affirmative. Anne, now wearing a sweater, mutters wryly, "Fat lot of good this will do for me now."

"What do you mean?" I ask.

Anne repeats, "Fat lot of good this will do for me now!" Several people laugh knowingly as Anne continues. "I've been investing as if I were walking around blindfolded for the past fifteen years. I have gone from stock to stock or mutual fund to mutual fund without an understanding of why I was making my trades. One time I even invested with a friend in a bridal shop that went bust. It's too late for me."

I don't need to say a word. Half the group jumps at the opportunity to straighten out their beleaguered friend. Bob sums up their comments best.

"We all have lots of investment time ahead of us," he says. "We can't do much about our past errors, but we sure can improve our investing habits going forward."

"True, we can be more careful to observe the four rules that we've listed," says Jack. "But there must be more to it than that."

"You're right, and the profitable ideas are yet to come," I reply. "Like the fifth rule—the *golden* rule—of successful investment, which says we need to make sure our portfolio is balanced with investments that complement each other."

Rule Five: Create a Complementary Combination of Investments

Jack leans forward. "Are you saying that we should diversify our portfolios?"

"Kind of," I say. "However, this concept goes much deeper that that. Keep in mind that earlier we said that the idea that a *diversified* portfolio is a *safe* portfolio is one of the investment industry's great half truths."

This time Anne steps in. "Yes, we talked about that in regard to mutual funds. We all agreed that your mutual fund might give you a diversified portfolio of stocks, but that's it—you just have *stocks*. So, if the equity market tanks, your entire portfolio is down."

Shaking his head, Jack says, "Don't I know it."

Lou has been quiet until now. "So is the goal to have a mix of investment categories in our portfolio?" he asks.

"You're getting close," I say, "but you're not quite there yet. The goal is to fill our portfolio with a mix of investment categories that *complement* each other."

Lou again speaks up. "So do we want investments that are all alike?"

Wow! Lou's comment makes me realize that I need to be sure we are all using the same definition of the term *complementary investment*. "Lou, let's say that you and a partner are going to start a new business that will manufacture widgets. You are an expert at widget design and manufacturing. With your background, what skills would you seek in a partner?"

Not missing a beat, Lou answers, "I want my partner to be a terrific widget salesperson."

"Right," I say. "Your partner's sales skills *complement* your design and manufacturing skills. If both of you were great salespeople or you both were expert designers and manufacturers, your new business might fail because the two of you do not have the full complement of skills necessary for success.

"A successful portfolio requires the same kind of balance. Complementary investments have features and characteristics that fit together like a jigsaw puzzle. Where one piece goes in, the other piece goes out. Like a lock and a key, like yin and yang. Just as you, the widget designer and manufacturer, and your salesperson partner *complement* each other."

Mark notices that not everyone is getting the concept, so he jumps in. "This really is a key point," he says. "Let me suggest an example. Let's say that you have decided to invest in two investment categories, and you want them to complement each other. A portfolio of T-bills and high-grade corporate bonds would not fit your needs because the two investments are not complementary. Both investments move in tandem—when one goes up or down in value, so will the other. An investment in an S&P 500 fund and the Fidelity Magellan Fund does not work either, because they, too, tend to move in tandem.

"However, a portfolio that has both stocks and real estate investments *does* work. Haven't you noticed that when stocks cool down, real estate heats up? As a result, these categories fit like our jigsaw pieces; when one loses value, the other is likely to rise. By choosing investment categories with performances that complement, rather than mirror, each other, we can even out our investment results—which is a good thing."

Jack moves to the edge of his seat. "I think I get it. By selecting two investment categories whose returns and risks don't correlate, you will be more likely to always have at least part of your money in the *hot market*."

"Right," I say. "I remember when I was a young man, in the summer my family would vacation in a beautiful resort town in northern Michigan. There was a wonderful restaurant in the town called the

Bayside Inn. The place had fantastic food and was always busy. Of course, I was there in the middle of the summer, when the town was buzzing with tourists.

"Several years after those family vacations, a friend and I were considering buying some property near that same town. (We didn't buy the land, and I still kick myself.) We drove up north on a cold, gray day in January to look at the acreage. After we were finished, I suggested a drive into town to have dinner at the Bayside. When we arrived, the restaurant was closed; there was a sign in the window that read, "See you next summer." My friend and I walked down the street, found a dingy bar, went in, and each ordered a beer and a hamburger. When the food came, we asked the man behind the bar about the Bayside.

"'Oh sure,' he said. 'That guy closes up every year just after Labor Day. He takes a few weeks off, then he goes down to St. Petersburg, Florida. He has a restaurant down there near the marina, I think it's called the Harbor Side Inn.'"

"That was a long time ago, and I never met the owner of the Bayside. However, you can be sure that with a restaurant in northern Michigan in the summers and another in St. Petersburg, Florida, in the winters, this was a guy who understood the concept of complementary investments."

Finding Balance and Creating Harmony

Carol and Bob both begin to speak. Carol pauses, but Bob keeps talking. "I've never considered this concept before now," he says. "The key is to build a portfolio where the investments harmonize. That's why successful investors have a portfolio that works year after year after year. They don't have a jumble of pieces and parts in their portfolio, but they've crafted a collection of investment types that work in harmony with each other. It's balance through the use of counterbalance!"

Jack jumps back into the conversation. "So you suggest that we should be invested 50 percent in stocks and 50 percent in real estate."

"Not quite," I say. "There are lots of complementary investment combinations that you can place in your portfolio besides stocks and real estate—investments that, as Bob said, harmonize. Let me suggest a few examples. The return and appreciation rates of bonds and stocks rarely correlate, so they are complementary investment categories. A person who holds a fixed annuity and mutual funds invested in emerging markets would have investments that don't correlate—hence that person's investments are complementary."

Lou looks up from his notepad and says, "So do we always need to have two investment categories in our portfolio?"

"There's no magic in holding two categories," I reply. "The best mix for you might be to have three or maybe four categories. What we do know for sure is that holding just one category is a poor idea.

"The highly successful Harvard endowment portfolio I mentioned earlier has fifteen categories of investments. Although few of us could hope to keep track of fifteen separate investment categories, the concept of complementary investment is valid for all investors."

Building Diversity Within a Narrow Range and Modern Portfolio Theory

How much money should we invest in each category? If we invest in two categories, should we have 50 percent in each? Or if we have three investments, should 33 percent of your money be in each? Again, there's no one-size-fits-all answer to this question. Your split will depend on a number of factors, including your comfort level with each investment category, your time horizon, and the amount we have to invest. A 1954 study by Harry Markowitz found that an investor using the two complementary investment categories (stocks and bonds) had the optimum combination of risk and reward with a twenty-eighty split—20 percent in bonds and 80 percent in a general portfolio of common stocks.

Many people credit Markowitz with developing the concept of modern portfolio theory (sometimes referred to as asset allocation). Markowitz undertook his work as a grad student at the University of Chicago in the 1950s. That research, which he continued to develop over many years, earned Markowitz the Nobel Prize in Economics in 1990 and planted seeds that encouraged research projects by many of the best economists around the globe. Their findings almost always support Markowitz's original thesis: The highest probability of long-term investment success belongs to portfolios that have more than one complementary investment category.

The room grows quiet as everyone starts to realize the importance of Rule Five: **Create a Complementary Combination of Investments.**

The night breeze has picked up, and both Mark and Jack have gone to the hall closet looking for sweatshirts. I start a fresh pot of coffee brewing. Lou brings some clean coffee cups out from the kitchen.

As Jack steps back on to the porch, he is pulling a well-worn maize-and-blue Michigan sweatshirt over his head. Still standing, he says, "What I don't understand is that earlier, we all agreed that we should invest in a narrow niche that we have taken the time to learn and understand. How does that fit with the concept of investing in multiple categories?"

"That's a critical point," I respond. "The reality is that successful investors have their money invested in more than one category. However, they develop their knowledge in a narrow area within each of those categories, and when they invest they stay in their slender niche. If real estate is one of their categories, they invest in only one type of real estate—the type that they understand. They don't dabble in renting single-family homes and at the same time build a regional shopping mall. If their investment category is stocks, successful investors will have taken the time to understand one stock selection process, such as how to find growth stocks or how to select value stocks. Inside each investment category, the successful investor works within a narrow focus, thus dramatically improving his or her results. Add to that the theory that successful investment portfolios will contain a complementary mix of two or more categories of investment, and we have a winning formula."

Improving Results by Smoothing Your Returns

Off to the side of the room, I catch Tim shaking his head. "What's wrong?" I ask.

"This is way too hard," he says. "Why don't we simply buy whatever is going to go up?"

Jack chimes in. "That's exactly the point. We can't be sure which investment categories will be the next to go up. We do know, however,

The Investment Wisdom of Markowitz, the Talmud, and Yogi Berra

I don't want to detract from the glory of a Nobel Prize winner, but in the interest of accuracy, I should point out that Harry Markowitz wasn't the first person in history to recommend that we keep a balanced portfolio of complementary investments. Consider this quote, for example.

Let every man divide his money into three parts, and invest a third in land, a third in business, and a third let him keep in reserve.

That pearl of wisdom came from the Hebrew Talmud, circa 1200 b.c. to 500 a.d.

If the Talmud isn't authority enough, in 1948, at spring training, a reporter asked New York Yankee Yogi Berra how the team would do that season. Yogi's response?

Making predictions is hard, especially when it involves the future.

Berra could have just as easily been talking about asset allocation. Investing would be a snap if we could invest in the rearview mirror. After the fact we are all brilliant and able to explain exactly what we should have done with our investment dollars. Berra's comment may seem whimsical; however, what he was saying is at the heart of building a good investment program. Another Berra comment is almost as insightful.

You can observe a lot just by watching.

Whether it's being said by Markowitz, Yogi, or the Talmud, the point is the same. Because we don't know which investment category will be the next hot opportunity, it's wise to have our investments in more than one area.

Sadly, even Markowitz failed to discover the exact balance of asset types that every investor should hold in a portfolio. The outcome of all the research in this area confirms that there is no exact formula. You can only find the perfect investment mix in hindsight. Looking forward, the best you can do is to create and maintain a complementary balance of investments.

that when one investment category is doing poorly, another is likely to be doing well. That means we have to be invested in more than one category at a time, and the categories that we select should be ones that do not correlate with each other. That's it?" Jack asks, turning to the room. "I have it?"

"You sure do," I answer.

Moving to the edge of his chair, Tim says, "I think I'm beginning to get it, but can we do just one more example?"

"Okay," I say, "but let someone else try their hand at it. Bob, what examples would you suggest?"

Bob seems to be ready for the question. "We've already said that the real estate market and the stock market don't move in tandem and so are complementary, right? Well, I think that the value of the U.S. dollar and the price of gold don't move in tandem, either. How about the price of energy and airline stock prices? Or interest rates and the stock of companies that carry a lot of debt? The list goes on and on."

"Okay," says Tim. "But tell me again—how is it that if you split your money between two investment categories that are moving in opposite directions, you don't end up at neutral?"

"That's a good point," says Bob, "but think about it this way. The assets we're talking about don't move in *opposite* directions. In fact, over time, they move in the same direction—*up*. They just don't move at the same time."

"Thanks, Bob, that is a great explanation," I say. "Let me address this using yet a different point of view. Tim, let's assume that there are only two investment categories—the stock market (we'll use the S&P 500) and real estate. Let's further say that you put 100 percent of your investment funds in one of those categories. Your investment plan is simple: When the category in which you are invested starts to cool down, you will switch all of your money to the other type of investment. You believe that this will always keep your money in the hot category. You reason that since there are only two categories, it won't be hard to select the next hot area."

Even though this sounds like a simple idea, the reality is that asset switching is damned difficult to do successfully. First, how do we know which investment category will be the next hot investment, and how do we tell if one ride is over and the other just beginning? Like they say, no one rings a bell to let you know. In hindsight, of course, it's easy. Today, we can all pick the exact day we should have sold our tech stocks or the exact day we should have bought energy futures.

But hindsight doesn't help in this decision. If we were to wait too long to switch our investment category, we would likely be selling near the bottom and buying the next investment near its top. In addition, we would keep paying transaction costs every time we shifted our investment portfolio.

If, however, we put part of our funds in stocks and part in real estate, the following things happen:

- We will always have at least some of our money in the hot investment category.

- We will have relatively even results.

- We will reduce the transaction costs of moving from one category to the next and back, over and over again.

- We dramatically reduce our risk of a major loss.

- We are unlikely to ever need to make a quick sale of an asset because we are under pressure.

- And we will sleep better.

Compounding "Balanced" Returns

"I see," says Tim, "but one last thing still bugs me. You said that by allocating our assets we would have relatively even results. So what? Why should I care if my investment results are smooth or if they are uneven?"

"This matter may seem small, but it can become a big issue very quickly," I respond.

There are two reasons to strive for even results from your investments:

- Unexpected things happen, and we don't know when we may need to cash out a portion of our investment. The more even the results of our investments, the less likely that we will be forced to sell at a bad time.

- Next—and this surprises lots of people—compounding a smooth return provides a higher return.

We have all seen one of those charts that show the compounded effect on $100 left in a savings account for an extended period of time. You know the kind that said something like, "If you had invested $100 when Columbus discovered America, today you would have a zillion dollars." Of course, you would also be dead. But, death aside, compounded returns are a good thing.

Now, here is the interesting part. Because a portfolio of complementary investments will have the effect of evening out our investment results, it also improves the effect of compounding. To prove this, let's compare different investments that have the same average return but different rates of return during the period that you are invested.

The following table compares the results of four sample portfolios. All the portfolios have an average return of 9 percent over a three-year period, but each has a different degree of variation in returns from year to year. Investor One has the smoothest returns, and Investor Four has the most uneven returns.

	Year 1 Return	Year 2 Return	Year 3 Return	Average Annual Return	Total Value of $100
1	9%	9%	9%	9%	129.50
2	20%	9%	-2%	9%	128.14
3	-2%	9%	20%	9%	128.18
4	4%	-12%	35%	9%	123.55

As you can see from this example, *the more even the average rate of return, the higher the compounded return.*

I know that the differences in these results seem small, but remember, this is only a three-year chart. The longer you expand the analysis, the greater the difference becomes. Also notice that the wilder the ride between high and low returns, the poorer the results. Compounding earnings is a good thing, and the steadier the return, the better.

"Over a ten-, fifteen-, or twenty-year investment period, this could have a meaningful impact," says Bob, as he jots down a quick note. "I never thought about the importance of trying to even out the results of my investments."

Taking Calculated Risks

Before moving on, I want to point out something that I think is very important and yet may have slipped by. "Earlier this evening, a few of you were concerned that we were going to build an investment plan that simply preached 'Be conservative,'" I say. "But I want you to notice two important elements of the rules we have been discussing:

1. Investors who follow the nine rules can safely accept greater risk than the typical investor because they have the safety net of holding complementary investment categories.

2. Investors who follow these nine rules also reduce the risks investments pose for typical investors because successful investors only invest in things that they understand.

"In other words," I emphasize, "successful investors don't refuse to take risks. They take *calculated* risks. Following the rules of successful investing gives you the freedom to take on risk wisely."

The level of enthusiasm of most of the people on the porch has certainly improved in the past half hour. It is clear that everyone is encouraged by the fact that the investment advice we're discussing comes, in part, from a Nobel Prize winner and that by following this advice, we can choose to take on greater risk if a good opportunity arises.

"Is that it?" asks Carol.

"Oh no," I reply. "Now that we have a solid foundation, we can take the next step followed by the most successful investors—and that's the step that makes them the most money."

5: The Rule That Makes the Most Money

"Money is plentiful for those who understand the simple laws which govern its acquisition."

—George Clason, author of *The Richest Man in Babylon*

"Thanks, but no thanks. You can count me out," says Jack as he leans far back in his chair. "I know that everything that is being said here tonight makes perfect sense, and I am sure that if we followed these steps we would all enjoy much better investment results, but I simply do not have time to constantly fiddle with my investments." The room grows quiet, and I realize that several others have been thinking the same thing.

I pause for a moment before responding, then say, "I can see how following the nine rules might sound complex and time-consuming, but I suspect that investing by these rules will be easier than the process you're using now, Jack."

So far, we have said that the following is true of successful investors:

1. They know what they don't know.

2. They identify an action that is profitable and then repeat that action again and again.

3. They understand that they must work through a learning curve.

4. They consider risk before return.

5. They strive to hold a mix of investments that complement each other.

Each of these rules actually serves to narrow our investing focus, not broaden it. Think about it: Selecting complementary investment categories usually requires a one-time decision, and it's not something we need to revisit each day, or week, or even each year. We make our investment decisions even easier by staying within a narrow subsection of the investment categories that we select. Following the Rules of Successful Investing makes our investments both more profitable and easier to manage.

Jack still seems a bit skeptical as I get ready to discuss the sixth rule. "Based on what you said, the next rule might *really* bug you, Jack," I say, "but it's the one that earns us the most money. Not everyone will want to take this step, and I understand that. But if you're willing (and able) to follow this rule, your investment returns can increase substantially."

Rule Six: Take Charge of One Investment

As we mentioned earlier, you can manage any investment yourself, or you can hire a professional and pay that person a management fee. The do-it-yourself approach saves you substantial fees and costs; however, it requires both knowledge and time:

	Self-Management	For a Fee
Equities	You can buy stocks	You can buy shares of a mutual fund
Real Estate	You can invest in real estate	You can buy units of a limited partnership or REIT
Business	You can operate your own business	You can invest in someone else's business

All too often people ignore fees when making investment decisions. They hear a small percentage number and think to themselves, "It's only 2 percent, it's so small it can't hurt." But investment fees can add up quickly.

"Let me give you an example," I say as I reach for a calculator and a legal pad. "Let's take a hypothetical investor named Joe. Age fifty, Joe has recently left his job. Joe's 401(k) has a $240,000 balance. Joe transfers the funds from the 401(k) to an IRA. The IRA management company that Joe is using charges a 1 percent fee that covers the management and all other costs of the investment. As fees go, this is very low. Joe makes no additional contributions to his account. He is a successful investor, and the gross earnings in his account earn an average of 12.5 percent per year. At age sixty-five, Joe closes the account. What will be the balance available?" After making some quick calculations, I write the following table on the legal pad:

Starting Amount	Time Invested	Earnings	Ending Balance
$240,000	15 years	12.5% gross	$1,404,126
$240,000	15 years	11.5% net	$1,148,301

As I pass the pad around the table, my guests' eyes widen in surprise at what they see. The 1 percent fee caused a quarter-million-dollar difference in the results. That amount is greater than the amount Joe had originally invested," I point out. "It is important to never lose sight of fees. Their impact is greater than most of us expect."

The best way to reduce fees is to be a do-it-yourself investor. Of course, it's unreasonable to think that any of us could be a successful do-it-yourself investor in every field. No one is skilled enough to be a knowledgeable real estate investor, stock market guru, retirement planning expert, *and* small business person all at the same time. Yet it's equally unreasonable to think that you can earn superior investment results if you pay heavy fees to others to make all of your investments for you. How to address the dilemma?

Selecting Your Specialization

To maximize results, many successful investors self-manage one of their investment categories. In most cases, these investors earn their best return from the category they self-manage, in part because that category is the one in which they have allocated the largest portion of their assets.

Rule Six is the big money maker for investors for a number of reasons. Not only does self-management save investors the costs of management fees, it also allows them to customize their portfolio to match their personal needs. For example, sales and purchases can be better timed to fit the investor's tax planning. Investors can employ more or less leverage to best align investments with their personal risk tolerance. The biggest benefit of self-management might be that it allows investors to continually expand their knowledge, contacts, and opportunities within their chosen category.

How do you select which investment category you will manage yourself? There are three questions you can answer to help you when making that choice:

- Which category of investing interests you most?

- In which category of investing are you most willing to invest your time, as well as money?

- If your holdings grew large enough, which area could you see becoming your occupation?

Knowing When to Pay Fees

Mark speaks up. "I better switch to decaf or I'll be awake for the next week." Everyone chuckles as Mark pours himself another cup of the high-octane coffee. "You know that what you're saying presents a bit of contradiction," he says.

"How so?"

"On one hand, you are saying that we should be invested in more than one category. Then you say that paying fees and costs are a bad idea. Lastly, you admit that it is next to impossible for one person to effectively self-manage more than one investment category. So, should we pay fees or not?"

"Point well taken," I admit. "Let's think of it this way. Unless a person is retired, hyperactive, and has a gallon-a-day Starbucks habit, he or she probably won't have the time or the energy to manage more than one investment area successfully. That's why most of us should select only a single investment category to self-manage.

"Now, as I mentioned earlier, it's likely that the self-managed category will be the area where we have our largest allocation. For the remaining one or two asset classes in our portfolio, we can select well-managed packaged products. Yes, we will be paying fees on part of our portfolio, but we'll be paying a fee to manage only half or maybe even less of our assets—which means that we will have reduced our overall management costs dramatically. I like to think of the fees I pay as the price of the added *safety of being invested in multiple investment classes.* Remember, most people are paying management fees on their entire investment portfolio. Using Rule Six, you will still pay fees, but only on a portion of your investments."

Building Around Your Core Strength

"Time out," says Jack, forming a capital letter "T" with two hands. "I'm not clear on how to select my complementary investments. Can we talk about that part again?"

"Jack, your confusion is understandable, because sometimes we do not execute the Nine Rules of Successful Investing in their numerical sequence," I say. "Here's what I mean. We learned in Rule Five to invest in complementary categories. In Rule Six, we learned that we should self-manage one of the categories of our portfolio.

"In practice, however, many people first execute Rule Six to determine what category they want to self-manage, and they then carry out Rule Five to select complementary investments to balance out their portfolio. That way, they are using their core investment as the starting point for their thinking."

Mark claps his hands loudly one time. "Eureka! That makes perfect sense. First, we need to think about the investment that we see ourselves managing—the core of our portfolio that we'll be living with on a week-to-week level. Once we know that, we can build the remainder of our investments to complement our core category. Choosing complementary investments should be a snap; we simply need to create balance by using investments that are a counterbalance to the investments in our core category."

You May Already Know Your Core Investment Category

I add, "I bet that everyone is further along in this process than you think. To find out, let me begin with a question for everyone here. Thinking about yourself, what category of investment would you want to manage?"

Anne is the first to respond. "My uncle bought a four-flat in Evanston about twenty years ago. Several years later he bought another about a block away and then another. About five years ago he sold all three buildings and bought a twenty-one-unit vintage apartment building near downtown Evanston, and just last month he bought an almost identical but slightly smaller building that was right across the street. I'd like to try something like that myself—building a portfolio of residential real estate in a middle- or upper-middle-class neighborhood."

Lou stands and walks toward the porch door. He takes a deep breath of the evening air and turns back to face the room. "Real estate may be fine for Anne, but I don't want to be a landlord even for a minute. I'll gladly pay someone else to do that. I love the stock market, and I think that now is the best time ever for market investors." The rest of the room looks at Lou, waiting for him to elaborate. "A few years back I read a book by Jeremy Siegel titled *Stocks for the Long Run*. The book's message stuck with me. Siegel clearly demonstrates that historically, stocks have outperformed every other investment type. Siegel even took his research all the way back to the early 1800s.

"Today," Lou continues, "the average investor has better information than anything available to even the most sophisticated professional investor of just ten years ago. There are hundreds of investment information sources to help investors select the stocks that fit their criteria, and most of them are available free or for a small subscription fee online. Of course, you have to spend the time to learn how to properly use the tools, but, boy, I don't think we've ever had so many investment aids at our disposal."

"We'll talk more about stock selection later," I interject.

"Plus," Lou finishes, "I think it would be great to get up each morning and make my trades for the day. I'd love to make a living doing just that."

"What about you, Carol?" I ask.

"I've already begun what I plan to do, and I am really getting the hang of it. I have been writing covered-call options. So far my return has been running about 18 percent a year. I have even had a few people approach me about managing some money for them. I am seriously considering starting a small investment management company after I retire in a few years."

"I would invest in myself," says Jack. "For the past ten years I have been buying the printing services for the publishing company where I work, and I enjoy that end of the business. I recently found a printing company for sale out near the airport. Running my own business is going to be my self-managed investment."

"Okay," I say, "just one more, or we'll be here all night. Mark, what investment would you want to self-manage?"

Without a pause, Mark says simply, "Real estate. But, unlike Anne, I have no interest in managing residential property. My interest is in going to those areas of the city that are just beginning to show signs of gentrification. Find and buy a down-at-the-heels building, fix it up, and sell it. I think that is where the bang for the buck is."

"This is great," I say. "You have created an almost ideal picture of exactly what we have been talking about. You each know what investment category you want to self-manage, and you know that you need to find at least one and maybe two complementary investment categories to balance your portfolio. All of you are closer to putting together that perfect portfolio than you may have thought only a few hours ago."

This Process Can Work for Anyone

I think that we are really making progress. Just then, I realize that both Bob and Tim have almost completely dropped out of the conversation. "What's up, guys? Don't you buy into this concept?"

Tim has the look of someone who is completely disconnected. After a long pause he says, "Some of you here tonight are sitting with comfortable 401(k) plans or maybe you have been socking away money in an IRA for years. Lou over there is getting ready to sell his business for a pretty penny. But I am not in your position. I never worked for a company with a 401(k) plan or any type of retirement program, and my savings are nothing to brag about. I guess this just isn't for me."

Before I can respond, Jack leans forward. "I think this line of thinking is for *everyone*. The size of the investments may change, but the concepts should work at every level of investment."

"Jack's right," I add. "Think about the risk-tolerance chart we made up earlier this evening. That chart works for everyone. No two people will place their maximum risk-tolerance point at the same level. As for thinking that some investments are priced out of your range, I can assure you that the richest person on this porch tonight could say the same thing. But no one should count themselves out. Investments are available at almost every level, and no matter how much you invest, the concept of investing in more than one category is still very valid."

"That makes me feel better," Tim says, "but what about the self-directed portion of the investment? That requires big dollars."

"I suggest that you should research the possibilities," I respond. "Carol's option-trading strategy can be started with as little as $1,500. The T-bills that we spoke of are sold in denominations of only $1,000. If you're thinking about a real estate investment, you might consider taking in a partner. Believe me, Tim, you are very much in this game."

Bob seems to have rejoined the conversation. He stands up and arches his back like someone who has been sitting for too long. "My situation is different. I'm fine with investing in more than one category, and I fully understand that I need to invest in areas that are complementary. The money isn't a problem, either—sure, I don't have as much money as I would like, but I have enough. The 'manage it yourself' part of this plan is where I have a problem. I see that it is the smart thing to do, but I simply don't have the time. This damned company I work for—they pay well enough but, boy, do they want their pound of flesh. I put in ten hours almost every day, and they have me flying off to somewhere almost every week. When I get home, I'm too tired to do much of anything. There is no way that I can take on self-managing an investment."

"Okay, Bob, but think about this. First, you know yourself better than anyone else, and if self-managing an investment is out of the question right now, so be it. So far tonight, we've talked about six rules for smart investing. If you can follow five of them, you're still better off than 99 percent of the investing public. Second, when things slow down for you, you'll be able to consider taking on the self-management of one of your investments. When that happens, what do you think you will choose?"

Bob's expression lights up as, still standing, he starts in. "About two miles from my office there's a long strip mall with a for sale sign in front of it. I called to find out the story. It seems that the owner died about four years ago, and the heirs have been arguing ever since. The mall is neglected. It looks dog-eared, the parking lot needs repair, and a few tenants have moved out. At the same time, home values in the area have been increasing. I'm sure that if that mall were cleaned up and managed properly, it could attract some better tenants at an increased rent. The best part is that there is no more open land in that area, so no other mall will come along to compete for tenants." After a short pause, Bob adds, "The project could be a real cherry, but I just can't commit the time that it would require."

I respond, "Here's my second suggestion. Bob, you have funding, and Tim is seeking funding. Perhaps the two of you should have an exploratory conversation. Tomorrow morning why not go to breakfast together. There's a place near here called, Betty's Restaurant, and they make great apple pancakes. Of course, you may discover that your business personalities or styles don't mesh as well as your investment goals, but it's worth a conversation. Both of you should keep in mind that there are lots people out there who are looking for funding or an active business partner."

Bob and Tim glance at each other. Bob says, "How is 7:30 AM for you?"

"Yeah, let's talk. Betty's Restaurant at 7:30 it is," replies Tim.

"It sounds like we have covered all the bases," says Lou.

"Almost," I reply. "There are just three little housekeeping rules left, and then we can tie everything together."

6: The Housekeeping Rules

He taught me about housekeeping. So, when we divorced I kept the house.

—Zsa Zsa Gabor, following her divorce from Conrad Hilton

Everyone is beginning to feel pretty good about tonight's discussion. Together, we have come to some important conclusions about how to invest. However, how do we keep the ball rolling once we get it started? This is where the three housekeeping rules come into play. A word of caution: Housekeeping can be hard work. With this in mind, we shift into the final, essential rules of successful investing.

Rule Seven: Keep It Simple

There is very little evidence to suggest that complex investments are more profitable than simple investments. In fact, a good deal of evidence tells us that the greater the complexity of the investment, the greater the risk of failure. (The more complex the investment, the more that must go right in order for it to succeed.) In addition, complex investments tend to carry a higher management fee burden.

Unfortunately, keeping your investments simple may be more difficult than you imagine. Why? Because investment salespeople like to sell us the broadest (read, most complex and, therefore, fee-laden) plans that their company offers. The complex—or, as they like to call them, "complete"—plans often pay the highest commissions or win the most company prize points that might land the salesperson that free trip to Hawaii or the new flat-screen television. My suggestion is this: No matter how bright the headline or how enthusiastic the salesperson, you should keep digging for the simplest plan with the fewest fees.

I know that simple investments are boring. I know that if you select only basic investments, you may not be the popular guest at dinner parties. I know that everyone will want to talk to Mr. Slick, who is telling a gathering crowd about his recent investment in "butterfly option spreads on foreign interest rates backed by mortgages on emerging-nation infrastructure." However, I also know that three years from now, Mr. Slick will be sitting at his desk with a twenty-one-inch pile of papers from the investment company, moaning, "I guess I should call my lawyer." We can also assume that Mr. Slick will be hoping that something (anything) of his investment will be left after legal costs.

Rule Eight: Trust Your Method and Stick with It

Before I can describe this rule, Anne speaks up. "Hold it. We already talked about trusting your method. I have something very close to this in my notes as Rule Two."

"Almost," I reply. "However, in Rule Two ("Invest, Succeed, Repeat") we talked about repeating a profitable action over and over again. Here, when we say 'Trust your method and *stick with it*,' we are talking about something different."

Just Look at History

Every investment category and method comes into and goes out of favor as the investment market cycles. For example, let's say that you are a value stock investor. You have taken the time to learn how to find and select value stocks from the numerous issues that are available. Let's also say that for the first two, three, or four years you invest in value stocks, things go great. Your value stocks outperform the market handsomely. In years five and six, however, growth stocks, not value stocks, outperform the market. Should you switch from value to growth investing?

To consider the wisdom of switching investment tactics, let's once again get a little help from our old friend Harry Markowitz, who wrote a study entitled "A Mathematical Analysis of Regression to the Mean." Regression to the mean, in an economic context, simply means that *over time, most investments return to their traditional rate of risk and reward.*

If the stock market typically goes up about 10 percent to 11 percent a year, it's likely that a period of growth greater than 10 percent to 11 percent a year will be followed by a period of growth that is less than 10 percent (maybe even a period of negative growth). The same can be said for all types of investments. If the growth in the value of real estate is typically 4 percent to 6 percent a year, it is reasonable to expect that a period of growth in real estate, when values are increasing faster, will be followed by a period during which values increase more slowly.

Markowitz wasn't the first to notice the concept of regression to the mean. In fact, the concept has been around almost forever. Ancient farmers wrote about a good harvest in one period being a predictor of a poor harvest in another period. Let's not forget other great words of wisdom on this topic by the band Blood, Sweat and Tears:

"What goes up must come down / Spinning wheel got to go round."

What does all of this have to do with our question about the wisdom of not switching our investment strategy from value stocks to growth stocks? We can look to history for guidance. The following table shows the comparative performance of value stocks and growth stocks over the nineteen-year period from 1986 to 2004.

Growth Stocks Versus Value Stocks: Best Performer, 1986–2005

1986	Growth	1996	Growth
1987	Even*	1997	Value
1988	Value	1998	Growth
1989	Growth	1999	Growth
1990	Growth	2000	Value
1991	Even	2001	Value
1992	Value	2002	Value
1993	Even	2003	Even
1994	Even	2004	Value
1995	Growth	2005	Value

In the years that are listed as "even," differences were too small to be meaningful for this comparison.

You Switch, You Pay

The obvious problem caused by switching investment methods is that we are likely to switch to the new method precisely as our old method is reviving. In addition, we will have a new learning curve to work through each time we switch. Finally, we may be required to pay sales or transfer costs.

Another important point hidden in these charts is that *both* growth-stock and value-stock investors significantly outperformed the typical trader, who bought and sold stocks without using a stock selection criteria or method. (The process of developing your own investment philosophy is discussed in Part 2.)

No matter how we examine this topic, the evidence leads to the same conclusion: Hopscotch is a wonderful game when played with chalk on the sidewalk, but investment hopscotch can be dangerous to our financial health.

Rule Nine: Rebalance Your Portfolio

If you see your dentist every six months and rebalance your portfolio every three months, you'll be able to keep smiling for many years to come.

It can be difficult to stick with your plan during those periods when your plan isn't performing well. As hard as that challenge may be, however, it's nothing compared to the emotional process of *rebalancing*.

After all, rebalancing seems counterintuitive. Let's say that you have $200,000 (we could just as easily say $20,000 or $20,000,000) to invest. You decide to invest 50 percent in the investment category you self-manage, 30 percent in asset class B, and 20 percent in asset class C. Hence, on day one, your portfolio is allocated as follows:

	Starting Allocation	Starting Balance
Asset Class A	50%	$100,000
Asset Class B	30%	$60,000
Asset Class C	20%	$40,000
Total		**$200,000**

You get started, and all goes well. Soon your portfolio has increased from $200,000 to $260,000. At that point, however, you find that the balance of your portfolio has changed.

	Starting Allocation	Starting Balance	Current Balance and Allocation
Asset Class A	50%	$100,000	$143,000 (55%)
Asset Class B	30%	$60,000	$91,000 (35%)
Asset Class C	20%	$40,000	$26,000 (10%)
Total		$200,000	$260,000

To rebalance the portfolio, you need to bring your investments back to their original percentage levels. In this case, you should sell some of asset classes A and B and buy more C. Why do this? Because asset classes A and B have been hot in the last period, there is an increased likelihood that they will cool in the next period. Historically, investment results regress to their traditional mean. The longer and hotter one period is, the longer and cooler will be the one that follows. Rebalancing keeps your investment results even, and we have seen how important that can be.

When you have finished rebalancing your portfolio, it will look like this.

	Allocation	Rebalanced
Asset Class A	50%	$130,000
Asset Class B	30%	$78,000
Asset Class C	20%	$52,000
Total		$260,000

Of course, in the real world, we rarely can make the rebalancing as exact as it is in the example. A reasonably close rebalancing will accomplish your goal.

I said that rebalancing may seem counterintuitive. This is because you will find yourself thinking that asset classes A and B are doing great. Why should you take money away from those winners and invest in an area that is struggling? Again, I suggest that you rely on what you have observed about markets. Hot markets cool down, and cold markets heat up.

My personal experience has shown me that this is the most difficult of the nine steps to follow. Nevertheless, rebalancing can offer handsome long-term benefits by reducing your risk due to overexposure to one investment type.

We now have discussed each of the Nine Rules of Successful Investing. Knowing the rules is the first step to investment success. Putting those rules into action is next.

7: Getting Started

We cannot do everything at once, but we can do something at once.

—Calvin Coolidge

I look at my watch. It is almost 2 a.m. The coffee is gone, the dish that had held two leftover slices of apple pie is clean. The bag of cookies is empty, and the bowls on the bar that once held nuts and chips have just crumbs left at the bottom. I notice that both Lou and Jack have started making notes listing their current investments. Bob and Tim are huddled together, talking about that shopping mall idea, and Mark is checking his list of the Nine Rules of Successful Investing against the list that Anne has been writing.

The nine rules are now in place. If we want to invest using the same mindset as the most successful investors, we have all the tools we need:

1. Know what we don't know, and then avoid investing in those areas.

2. Identify an action that is profitable and then repeat that action again and again—even if it becomes a little boring.

3. Understand that there is a learning curve, and expect to make some mistakes along the way.

4. Consider risk before we consider return because risk is real.

5. Strive to hold a mix of investment categories that complement each other, seeking investments that balance each others' performance.

6. Self-manage one of our investment categories to improve performance and reduce management costs.

7. Keep things simple as another method to improve results and lower management costs.

8. Stick with your method of investing, even when it does not generate the best results during a period or two.

9. Regularly rebalance your portfolio. Even though it is difficult, it's worth the effort.

Let's be realistic. Although each of the Nine Rules of Successful Investing makes good sense, when taken as a whole, the list can be daunting. Few of us are prepared to run out tomorrow and reshuffle our entire investment portfolio, close old accounts, transfer funds, and initiate new actions. So what should we do? Well, like all investors, we have three options:

• Do nothing, and continue as we have in the past.

• Start to employ at least some of the nine rules.

• Wait until we can do everything before we do anything.

Of course, everyone knows that the second option is the most reasonable. As someone once said, "The greatest obstacle to progress is the delay we cause by waiting for perfection."

Happily, we do not have to stumble over that obstacle. Improving our investment success is a process, not an event. Planning and starting that process can seem like a major task, but it becomes much more manageable if we think of it as a series of simple steps we can take one at a time.

Choosing First Steps

The nine rules are now ours, and we can use them as we see fit for the rest of our investing career. But how do we get started? We all know the old saying, "The longest journey begins with a single step." That's great advice for taking control of your investment process. If you can look at the nine rules and select just one to immediately put into action, you will have taken the first step toward improving your investment decisions. Further, your investment results will be greater than those of the millions of people who follow none of the rules.

If you are able to follow *two* of the rules, your results will be better yet. In two or three months, you can come back to the list and add a third rule to your investment management style, then a fourth, and so on. Expect it to take a year or eighteen months to incorporate all rules that you will use. Remember, success takes time. Use that time to get comfortable with each step as you move forward.

You may find it helpful to map out a plan for putting the rules into action. Here is my suggestion:

1. List your current investments.

2. Make notes defining your investment goals/needs. Include information about risk tolerance and your time horizons. For example, at this time in your investment career, are you most interested in growth, with less need for current income? Or is your goal to have higher current income, and are you willing to accept lower long-term growth?

3. Decide if you have the time or desire to self-manage one of your investment categories. If so, choose that category—it will be your core investment.

4. After choosing your self-managed category, select at least one and maybe two investment categories that complement your core category to balance out your portfolio. For most investors, steps 3 and 4 will involve some combination of equities, real estate, fixed investments, or business investment. Some may consider commodities or foreign investments

5. Look at the list of assets you wrote down in step 1. Is the balance of your present portfolio anywhere close to the portfolio you listed in steps 3 and 4? If not, it is time to start making the changes needed to align your portfolio with your goals. This step will dramatically reduce your risk and improve your investment results.

6. Now that you have planned your work, it's time to work your plan. You do this by personally managing one of your investments and regularly monitoring the balance of your portfolio.

7. Rebalance your portfolio as needed. Some people like to rebalance when the values in the various investments are 5 percent or more out

of alignment with the original plan. Other people like to rebalance once a quarter. (Either method is fine.)

Using these steps most of us will be able to write our basic plan in just a few days. However, as I said earlier, you should expect it to take a year or more to put your plan completely in action. Don't be impatient with this process. The time you spend developing and implementing your plan is one of the most profitable investments you will ever make.

The Hard Part Is Over

Jack has begun to help straighten up the porch, gathering the empty coffee cups and glasses, when suddenly he stops what he is doing. He turns to the room and says, "Hold it. We've just spent half the night talking about money, and even though I'm now smarter about how to manage my investments, I am as bewildered as ever about the nuts and bolts of investment products."

"Yep, that's an important observation, Jack," I respond. "Let's think back to the beginning of the evening. We started our conversation by saying that *how you invest has a greater impact on your success than what you invest in.* Our discussion this evening focused on the most important aspect of successful investment—knowing *how* to invest."

"What we have really been talking about here tonight is money management. That is the critical skill that the average investor overlooks. Whether we're sitting down at the tables in Las Vegas, getting ready to launch a new business, or taking control of our investments, we can't succeed over the long term unless we know how to manage our money. Sadly, most gamblers, new business owners, and investors don't bother learning and following the critical rules that we have talked about this evening. That might be why most gamblers lose, many new businesses fail, and most investors are disappointed with their returns.

"But we're no longer in the pool of 'average' investors. After tonight, our approach to investing will never be the same. We know the Rules of Successful Investing, and we have a plan for following them. So let's congratulate ourselves. We have just completed the most important step to investment success."

I start to gather up my things with every intention of heading up to bed.

"Not so fast," Jack calls out. "I agree that we have come a long way toward understanding the 'theory' of successful investing. But I think many of us still have a concern about how to take that first practical step. Sure, you said that we may want to buy stocks, but I still don't know how to select the stocks I want for my portfolio. You suggested real estate investments, but here too I don't know how to take my first steps."

Clearly, I can't argue with Jack. He makes an excellent point. But what to do? It's after 2 A.M., and everyone is tired. Tomorrow after breakfast we all plan to drive back to the city.

"I've got an idea," says Lou. "This is the last weekend in May. Those who want to can return here on the last weekend of each month for the rest of the summer. Each month we can tackle the nuts and bolts of a different type of investment."

"That's a good idea," agrees Carol. "With each discussion we can see how to apply the Nine Rules of Successful Investing."

Before I can respond, Lou says, "Okay, next month I'll bring the steaks and drinks for the barbeque."

Jack is right behind him. "Good idea, I'll bring everything for the July meeting."

Bob chuckles as he glances in my direction. He cups his hands around his mouth. "*All aboard!* This train is leaving the station!" After a little laughter Bob adds, "I'm going fishing the third week of August. If all goes as I expect, I can bring back a fresh catch for the third weekend meeting."

Mark and Anne are laughing as the thought of having a monthly discussion group takes shape in a matter of minutes. Anne volunteers, "I'll manage the food and drinks in September."

Then Mark asks an important question: "Does everyone really want to do this?"

"Yes. Sure, absolutely," come the responses.

"Okay," I say. "Then if we are all going to go to the effort of planning the meetings and giving up part of a weekend each month, we all need to remain vigilant as to the original intention of this discussion. The real purpose of the monthly get-together is to improve our investment results as we all plan for the future. We started tonight with a critical premise: *No amount of savings can overcome the handicap of poor investment performance.* Hence, our futures depend more on the performance of the money we already have than on the few extra dollars that we can save each month."

The room gets suddenly quiet as everyone considers the consequence of a failed investment plan. Then, Mark, in his best "Mr. Organization" style and with BlackBerry in hand, quickly reads the dates of each coming assembly and who has volunteered to be the "chief cook and bottle washer" for each weekend. He turns to me and says, "Dennis will e-mail us the topic for each weekend so we can be ready to make the most of the discussion."

Everyone is smiling except me. Sure, I love the company, but this may have turned into more than I bargained for. Twenty minutes later, as I try to slip quietly into bed, I accidentally wake my wife.

"Did you accomplish everything you wanted tonight?" she asks.

"Sure, sure. By the way, did we have anything important planned on the last weekend of the month for the rest of the summer?" I ask.

"No, not that I know of. Why?"

To: Lou, Carol, Mark, Anne, Bob, Tim, and Jack
From: Dennis
Here's our list of investment topics for the monthly meetings:

June: How to generate profits by selecting stocks and writing options.

July: When and how to use insurance-based investments and fixed investments; how to avoid market fraud.

August: How to make a business investment that will earn maximum reward with minimum risk.

September: How to make money on real estate—it's not only for the rich.

See you on the porch,
Dennis

Part 2:

**MAKING MONEY WITH STOCKS,
OPTIONS, AND FIXED INVESTMENTS**

8: The Simple Recipe for Stock Market Success

Some Day Warren Buffett Will Be Reading about Me!

Jack's idea for monthly visits seems to have had a significant impact. Instead of filing away the concepts that we had talked about as "a good idea that we might get to someday," the realization that there would be monthly gatherings makes us all more attentive to the ideas that we discussed in May. For example, as we sit on the porch, I see that everyone has made an itemized list of his or her current portfolio. Many even have little notes next to some of the names on their list of investments. I glance down at Jack's list and see that next to one of his items he has written, "Why in the hell did I ever buy this junk? What was I thinking"? Although not everyone has been that hard on themselves, many have come to realize that they own investments that are long past their prime.

After some conversation and complaints about golf games, the high price of gas, and the poor repair of the roads, it is time to get down to work. This month we plan to focus on the stock market.

"It's a fact," I begin, "that in the long term, common stocks have outperformed almost any other investment that you could have made. Of course, the 'long term' referenced in this statement includes the years extending from 1925 to the present."

Here is another fact: Many people who invest in the stock market have disappointing results because they don't follow the basic steps to investment success. Instead, they invest their money and hope to get lucky. It could happen. The stock market, like any investment, goes through a series of cycles, and that means that once in a while even a blind squirrel can find an acorn.

In December 1982, a financial columnist for a large newspaper decided to have a stock-picking contest. He invited readers to submit a list of five stocks they believed would perform well in the following year. At the end of the year, the results of each entry's hypothetical investment would be calculated, and the winner and his or her picks announced, along with the identity of a mystery contestant.

Entries came flooding in. Stock brokers entered the contest, as did financial analysts, a professor of finance from a local university, professionals, amateurs—even the writer of the business column placed his entry in the pool.

As promised, the special contestant was eventually revealed. It was the reporter's pet parakeet. It seems that at the start of the contest the columnist had lined the bottom of the bird's cage with the newspaper's financial page. He then allowed the bird to "select" five stocks. The bird's entries were treated just like the rest of the contestants. While the parakeet did not win, she did place in the top half. From these results, we can deduce that about half of investors in the contest underperformed bird droppings.

Yet many investors do succeed year after year. We all know some of the legendary names, such as Benjamin Graham, Warren Buffet, and Peter Lynch. Beyond their investment success, these great investors share one thing in common: They each have an investment philosophy that they rely on, year after year.

At this point, new investors may be saying, "Okay, what's the philosophy that the successful investors use? I'll use the same one." The surprise answer is that each of these investors has a unique philosophy, and sometimes those philosophies contradict each other. It turns out that simply *having* and following an investment philosophy is the key to successful stock market investing.

Notice, I did not say that we need a trading *technique*. Trading techniques are great fun (to view from a distance). They are printed in books, magazines, and passed around at parties. Here's one that keeps coming back every few years:

"If a stock goes up two days in a row and down the third day, you should buy the stock if it is trading higher than the previous day's close thirty minutes following the opening on the fourth day."

Don't laugh. This is a real trading technique, and I know people who have used it. Take it from me: Techniques are not the answer to reliable stock market success. Hoping that a trading technique will make you rich without having an investment philosophy as a foundation is like predicting the outcome of your day by reading your horoscope. Sure, by sheer coincidence, a horoscope might accurately depict some event that takes place in your day, just as the same coincidence might give a trading technique a short run of success. However, most people should be unwilling to stake their future on coincidence.

The frustrating fact about most trading techniques is that some of them work *in the short term*. Even more frustrating is investors' tendency to fall for these gimmicks. If a trading technique works just two times in a row, it will be written up in 100 different magazines, and thousands of people will follow it. In the long term, however, these techniques offer about as much real value as do horoscopes. To be successful, we need an investment *philosophy*. You're going to learn some of the most successful investment philosophies tonight, and perhaps you'll make one of them your own.

"Philosophy," says Bob. "I didn't bargain for this. You're not going to tell me that we have to study transcendental meditation and sit in the lotus position, are you?"

"Not that kind of philosophy," I say. "I'm talking about an investment philosophy. And don't worry that you won't be able to find a philosophy with which you feel comfortable. Some of the most successful investment philosophies are uncomplicated and easy to follow. The most important factor is learning and understanding your stock selection philosophy and allowing your philosophy to guide your investment decisions.

"Achieving your goal will require a bit of your time and attention. If you're willing to do more than just sit back and wait for success to fall into your lap (or onto the financial page, so to speak), let's move on. What we say tonight can be the road map to stock market ecstasy.

"Here's one of the most important guidelines to follow in developing your philosophy: *Long-term investment results are more dependent on the actions of the investor than on the actions of the market.*

"Most market observers break down stock market trading into three or four basic philosophies. We will focus on the basic three. Each has merit. Investors using each have succeeded in the past and will succeed in the future."

Market Philosophy One—The Efficient Market

The efficient market hypothesis: This philosophy's roots go back to 1901, when mathematician Louis Bachelier wrote a Ph.D. dissertation, titled "The Theory of Speculation," that put forth a radical concept. Bachelier said, "The mathematical expectation of a speculator is zero." Bachelier's work received almost no attention for several reasons:

- Bachelier was an unknown.

- His ideas were heresy to active investors.

- He wrote his paper in French and it was not translated into English for almost sixty years.

Eugene Fama made the next major contribution to the efficient market concept in a 1965 article, titled "Random Walks in Stock Market Prices," which was followed by Burton Malkiel's 1973 book, *A Random Walk Down Wall Street.* These works theorize that because all investors buy and sell for their own reasons, every trade is a random event; short-term market value changes are therefore unpredictable, and studying market fundamentals is a waste of time and effort. But since the market has risen in value over time, the best way to participate successfully is to "buy and hold the market."

In the early 1970s, a University of Chicago graduate student named Rex Sinquefield read the above-mentioned publications. The concepts motivated Sinquefield to do some heavy number crunching, which led him to make further refinements to the earlier works. This in turn led to what we know today as the efficient market hypothesis. Get ready. Here it is:

Most investors fail to outperform the market.

It may not seem so revolutionary today, but Sinquefield's statement was groundbreaking. Notice he did not say some investors, but "most investors." Not just amateurs, but amateurs and professionals alike.

Like the theory itself, the reasoning behind the efficient market hypothesis is simple. Investors seek to buy stocks that are undervalued and to sell stocks that are overvalued. But the theory holds that the *stock market is efficient.* Thus, all securities are properly priced. As a result, there are no overpriced or underpriced stocks available to investors. When an investor is fortunate enough to marginally outperform the market, the management and transaction costs offset that performance advantage.

Sinquefield makes some very strong points. First, with the exception of undisclosed insider trading (which is illegal), every piece of data about every company is available for everyone. The efficient market hypothesis in part, rests on this fact. If everyone has the same information, the same news, and the same economic framework in which to invest, it is unlikely that any individual can beat the market.

"Ridiculous," says Jack. "We're smarter than the average guy."

"Okay," I respond, "but think about this. There are 6 billion people on planet Earth. Can we be smarter than the sum of the knowledge of 6 billion people? How many times have you seen or heard that something good or something awful happened to a company in the middle of the night, only to find that the full effect of that news had been factored into the stock's price before the market opened the next morning? In other words, you do not and you *cannot* know something that no one else knows. To this day, Sinquefield continues to develop astute data that support his original findings: *Most investors, professional or amateur, fail to achieve performance better than that of the general market.*"

Several things happened following the publication of Sinquefield's findings. First, most of the press ignored his work, just as most of the public had ignored Bachelier's work three-quarters of a century earlier. Sinquefield's words were a profanity to the professional investing community, who considered it damned un-American to even think such thoughts. "We are smarter," they reasoned, "we are professionals, and we can and always will rise above the crowd." Yet here was a grad student from the University of Chicago saying that he had hard, statistical evidence that proved them wrong.

Sinquefield was lucky. He somehow escaped being tarred and feathered by an angry mob of portfolio managers and landed a job at the right place at the right time. American National Bank in Chicago had an investment management division and a few mutual funds. Their funds' performance was lackluster at best, and the bank was looking for a new idea. Along came Sinquefield. As a rookie employee, he was able to convince the bank management to give his concept a try. That concept was most simple: Just invest in the market. Don't pay high-cost investment managers. Don't pay for high-cost research. Don't try to time getting in and getting out. Simply buy the market. (Today, we might say "Buy the S&P 500 or the Russell 3000." However, in the early 1970s, these indexes were not fully matured.)

The next development really iced the deal. Sinquefield devised a method whereby the bank had to buy only about 110 different stocks to mimic the results of the market. In August, 1973, American National Bank launched the first index fund. Six weeks later, Wells Fargo in San Francisco launched its index fund. The industry was born. The idea of settling for an average return was so foreign, so "un-American," that it was two full years before a single major investor could be attracted to the fund. In 1975, New York Bell (remember when we had local Bells?) invested $40 million of its pension funds with American National Bank. This investment was like a stamp of approval. Money began to flow in, and today almost 30 percent of all pension funds are held in index funds.

Did Rex Ever Get Paid for His Work?

Frequently people who start a revolution don't cash in on their groundbreaking work, but we don't need to worry about Rex Sinquefield. He seems to be doing fine. At the end of 2005, he retired from his day-to-day work at Dimensional Fund Advisors, a company he founded in Santa Monica, California, and which manages $70 billion in assets. Today, Sinquefield continues his research and travels with his family. (Nice going, Rex.)

Let's not forget Eugene Fama, who laid the groundwork for Sinquefield's efficient market hypothesis. Fama is now a director of Dimensional Fund Advisors and earns a royalty for his contribution to the concept.

Both Sinquefield and Fama have been mentioned as possible Nobel Prize candidates in the field of economics.

Market Philosophy Two—Value Investing

"Value investing—that's for me," says Lou. "You're in good company," I reply. Value investors are the bargain hunters of the investment world. The father of value investing was the respected, almost-revered Benjamin Graham, who immigrated to the United States from England at the turn of the twentieth century. Today, Graham's two landmark texts—Security Analysis, first published in 1934, and The Intelligent Investor, published in 1949, both co-authored with David Dodd—are still in print and selling nicely.

Some of Graham's continued popularity comes from the fact that he was a mentor to a young Warren Buffett, one of today's best-known value investors. Buffett continues to this day to frequently cite the works of Ben Graham and refers to him as one of the greatest thinkers the market has ever known.

What are value stocks? Using a strict definition, "value stocks are the stocks of companies with a net asset value per share greater than the market price of the stock." The following table shows a pure value stock, as defined by Ben Graham. The company has 1 million shares outstanding, and the net asset value per share is greater than the market price per share. The *value* in this example results from the fact that you can buy this stock below the value of it net assets.

Value Stock—A company with 1,000,000 shares outstanding

Total net assets is $20 million	Net assets per share equals $20
Market price per share is $12	You can buy the stock for $12 per share

Following Graham's theory, investing in this stock would hold almost *no risk*. Even if the company were to go out of business, a liquidation of the assets could generate a profit to the investors.

There is a catch to Graham's original theory of value investing, which became apparent over time. Graham developed his original work in the 1930s, when the nation was in a depression and the stock market was low, low, low. In that environment, and with some research, it was easy to find companies with stock selling at prices below the company's net asset value. By the mid-1960s, however, finding such companies had become difficult.

Today, the definition that investors use to identify a value stock is more liberal. Various factors may be used, such as identifying stocks with a lower-than-average stock market price compared to company sales (called the price-to-sales ratio) or a lower-than-average stock price when compared to net assets (called the price-to-book ratio) or lower than average price-to-earnings ratio. The idea is to identify stocks that appear inexpensive based in a measurable metric.

In investing, everything moves in cycles. Using his hypothesis, Ben Graham would have missed the stock market's meteoric rise during the Internet craze of the late 1990s. Of course, he also would have missed the market's slide that followed. Value funds showed excellent performance in the years from 1989 to 1996 and 2001 to 2004.

What happened to Ben Graham?

After a long and successful career as an investor, Graham retired from active trading and took up residency at Columbia University, where he taught market theory. He continued to revise his two published books almost until his death in 1976 at age eighty-two. His market ideas are still being followed, and remain relevant for every investor.

Market Philosophy Three—Growth Stocks

"Value, shmalue—give me growth!" So say the growth-stock groupies. These investors ask why they should care if the underlying book value' or dividend payout rate is high or if it's low, when the only factor that really matters (to them) is that a stock is increasing in value.

"Now you're talking," says Bob. "That's what I want."

"Really?" I respond. "Let's think about this for a moment. I have seen too many people run off looking for a stock they think has growth opportunities, only to end up buying at the market high."

"The problem may be with the name *growth stock*, which causes the amateur investor to seek stocks that have been rising in price. The person buys the stock based on the assumption the price rise will continue. Well, here's a news flash. Trees don't grow to the sky, and stocks don't just keep going up."

"So what should we be looking for?" asks Bob.

"The more reliable approach is to identify *growth companies*. This isn't a guarantee, but it will greatly improve your long-term results," I respond.

The experienced growth-stock professional seeks companies whose earnings and/or sales are growing faster than others in their industry.

Dividend payment is, at best, a secondary consideration for growth investors.

The growth-stock hypothesis is widely advocated. Even the cautious National Association of Investors Corporation (NAIC) encourages this method of investing. One of America's most successful money managers is Richard Driehaus, a dyed-in-the-wool growth-stock practitioner. In 1980, Driehaus founded Driehaus Capital Management, where he still works today as the company's chief investment officer. The Driehaus funds manage $2.7 billion and have enjoyed top-flight returns. The Driehaus Small Cap Growth fund turned in an aggregate return of 9,352 percent between January, 1, 1980, and March 3, 2005.

The growth-stock investment concept states that investors should look for companies with sales and earnings that are growing faster than others in their peer group. For now, you may just want to identify companies that display growing sales and earnings. As you become a more experienced growth-stock investor, you can begin to identify the "quality of the earnings." To determine the quality of a company's earnings you would be interested in learning:

- If sales are really growing, or is the company selling its core assets and milking its product line?

- Is there reason to believe that the growth can continue? Are there new products on the horizon? Does management have a solid and executable plan for growth?

- What is management's plan for their money? Can the company's earnings be reinvested in the business profitably? Are there acquisition opportunities?

One of the things that many investors like about growth investing is that once you have your growth investment criteria clearly defined, you also know when to sell. The when-to-sell signal is sounded when one of your "buy" criteria is no longer being met.

Applying Rule Seven

Having a clear understanding of your investment philosophy fits into the Nine Rules of Successful Investing. Once you have selected a philosophy, you eliminate countless distractions when making your stock selection. As Rule Seven reminds us, "Keep it simple."

Your Philosophical "Fit"

"Okay," says Anne, "now the million-dollar question: Which philosophy is right?"

"Anne, I understand that seems to be the big question, but it's not," I respond. "Efficient market hypothesis, value investing, and the growth stocks philosophy are all valid strategies."

You might even be drawn to other market philosophies, such as the behaviorist philosophy, of which the very successful Josef Lakonishok, founder of LSV Asset Management, is a proponent. According to this philosophy, most investors act as a pack, driven by either fear or greed. More informed investors are able to succeed by exploiting weakness in the thinking of the herd.

No matter what philosophy you are considering, remember that almost every major investment philosophy is right at one time or another. In most years, index funds (an example of efficient market hypothesis) outperform the bulk of investors. Yet index funds rarely place in the top quadrant of performers in any year.

Can you outperform the index? Yes. Every year there are investors who outperform the average. The first step toward that success is getting a good grasp of an investment philosophy. Combine your consistent stock market investment approach with the Nine Rules of Successful Investing, and you will hold the winning hand.

"You see," I add, "many of the people who are disappointed in their long-term results from their stock market investments can be divided into two camps:

1. They have no philosophy to help guide their decisions, so each trade is little more than a random event.

2. They start out with a philosophy but keep changing their mind with each little market shift. These people play philosophy hopscotch.

To succeed, don't forget Rule Eight, "Trust Your Method and Stick with It."

Carol gets up for a cup of coffee, and almost everyone follows.

9: Pinpointing Stock Market Winners

It's More Than Eeny-Meeny-Miney-Mo

As we return, Bob remains standing, and with a self-confident air he announces, "I finally did it."

"Did what?" Mark asks.

"I have started Weight Watchers. After talking about it for ten years, I finally went to a meeting," says Bob.

"I guess that my teasing got to you. How much have you lost?" asks Mark.

"So far, about $80," says Bob. "I paid some fees and bought a few books. I plan to start the diet on Monday; right now I'd like you to pass me the potato chips."

We all laugh. Then, with potato chips in hand, Bob says, "Come on. I still don't know how to select a stock."

"Okay, Bob, here it is," I say.

If you dread the thought of managing your stock market investments, relax, take a deep breath, and repeat after me: *It's not that hard.* In fact, self-managing your stock market investments is a lot easier than it has ever been. Why? Because the data that you need for that task has been carefully recorded and organized. Other than baseball statistics, I can think of no other human endeavor that has been so well documented.

As recently as ten years ago, locating and retrieving relevant stock market data in a usable form was a task best suited for market analysts and grad students. Today, the Internet has made almost every iota, gram, and speck of data instantly available to anyone with a computer and an online connection. Every morsel of information is tracked, refined, and updated minute by minute. Updates are available at no cost from most online brokers or for a modest fee from a subscription service. (See pages 91–97 for a list of good online data services.)

As we said, choosing a stock market investment philosophy is the first step toward success. Once that is complete you are ready to move on to the next two essential steps in that process:

- Choosing a market sector(s) for investment
- Selecting individual stocks within the sector(s)

No matter what investment philosophy you choose, you will rely on market indicators that act as the triggers you look for to advance your action. We call these indicators *selection filters*. There are more stock-selection filters than we could ever talk about in a single night, so we will focus on those filters that we know to be both accessible and reliable. No one uses—or should use—every available stock selection filter when selecting trades. I suggest you consider the wide variety of selection filters available to you as your toolbox and choose from it those indicators that seem the most compatible and useful with your investment philosophy and style.

Selecting the Target Industries for our Investment

Before we choose individual stocks, we need to decide which industry or market sector offers the best potential. Two factors can influence this decision: our own observations, and hard data.

From observation, you may have an idea as to what might be the next growth industry. Do you believe that everyone is going to buy a new HDTV? If so, you might consider investing in the electronics manufacturing and electronics retailing sectors. Do you predict that there will be a seismic shift from gasoline-powered cars to hybrid vehicles? In that case, you might believe that manufacturers of the electronic controls used to operate these new cars make a great industry in which to invest.

Never underestimate the power of your own personal observations. The legendary investment manager, Peter Lynch, has repeatedly said that watching social trends is his key investment selection indicator.

Still, many of us prefer to base our investment decisions on something more substantial. If you would rather rely on hard numbers, you can turn to *sector rotation data.* Sector rotation information tracks the flow of money into and out of stock market sectors. Sector rotation statistics are updated daily and are widely available on a subscription basis through several online services. We can use this data to learn where the money flow in the market is heading and thus achieve significant improvement in our trading selections and results.

Here's an example. Let's say that our online market information service points out that for the past two weeks, the owners of tech stocks have been *net sellers.* The service also tells us that money is flowing into the shipping and transportation sector. Hence, the shipping and transportation sectors have *net buyers*.

In this example, the market is shouting (to those who are listening) that it might be a good idea to lighten up tech stock holdings and consider buying stocks in the shipping and transportation sector. At the very least, if we currently hold investments in the tech sector and in the shipping sector, we may want to sell some of our tech, or *underweight* our tech portfolio, and add to, or *overweight*, our holdings in shipping.

Is sector rotation information important? In 2004, the S&P 500 had a fine year, growing by 20.3 percent; however, the growth was uneven. While an investor who held the full S&P index in, for instance, an S&P 500 mutual fund, might have been happy with the 20.3 percent return, some sector picking could have produced much better results. For example, the investor who kept an eye on sector rotation might have known to stay out of, or at least underweight his commitment to, the consumer staples sector, which only grew at 5 percent, and the telecommunications services sector, which lost 7 percent. An observant investor would, instead, have shifted his holdings to information technology (overweighting his portfolio), which was up 64 percent, and materials, which was up 66 percent.

Investing in Exchange-Traded Funds (ETFs)

If you are not interested in making individual stock selections, you can eliminate that step completely and just be a sector investor. You simply use your personal observations and sector rotation data to choose industries that you believe have the best potential for growth, and then invest in an exchange-traded fund (ETF) representing that sector.

What is an ETF? Think of a sector index fund that trades like a stock. ETF shares trade on exchanges. Their price is set by supply and demand. Because an ETF trades like a stock, they can be bought and sold during the same day and are highly liquid. ETFs can be bought on margin, and, like stocks, they may be sold short. (Short selling is covered in detail on page 81.) ETF management fees are generally less than those of a mutual fund. The management fees charged by ETF's range from a low of one tenth of 1 percent to a high of about 1 percent.

The first ETF began in 1993 and represented the stocks in the S&P 500. This ETF was soon nicknamed Spiders (based on its ticker symbol, SPDR). Spiders quickly became popular and opened a floodgate of new ETF offerings. Today, there is an ETF for every imaginable sector. Some have specific names (for instance, Russell 1000), others are collections of stocks grouped by economic sector (for example, the Internet) or by country.

A Partial List of Exchange-Traded Funds

S&P 500	Dow Jones Averages	Chemicals
Basic Materials	Energy	Healthcare Financial
Technology	Utilities	Australia
Brazil	Belgium	Canada
France	Germany	Hong Kong
Italy	Japan	Malaysia
Mexico	Netherlands	Singapore
Spain	S. Korea	Sweden
Switzerland	Taiwan	UK
Russell 1000	Rus 1000 Growth	Rus 1000 Val
Russell 2000	Rus 2000 Growth	Rus 2000 Val
Russell 3000	Rus 3000 Growth	Rus 3000 Val
Europe Mid Cap	S&P Small Cap	S&P Mid Cap
NASDAQ 100	Internet	Real Estate

"I'm really beginning to get it," says Anne. "It's a matter of steps from the broad to the specific. First, we choose our macro investment philosophy. Maybe we want growth or value. That choice remains consistent.

"Then, we select the industry groups we think offer potential. As the flow of money in the stock market is an ever-changing tide, we will always be checking for market rotation to be sure we are looking for stocks in the right sectors. I guess the next step would be selecting the specific stocks to buy."

"Anne, I couldn't have said it better," I reply.

Mark says, "You know, almost every one of the nine rules is showing up here. First, we must embrace the learning curve, as we learned in Rule Three. Then, by checking to see which sectors are growing, we help avoid losing money, from Rule Four. And because we are do-it-yourself investors, we also take charge, as we learned in Rule Six."

Selecting Individual Stocks

After you have chosen your target industry sectors, you could simply invest in those sectors using exchange-traded funds and do just fine. However, if you want to shoot for the moon, you need to take the next step and learn to select the best individual stocks within your target industries. Few investments can outperform the hot stock in the hot industry. Here are just two examples:

- A 1980 investment of $5,000 in Wal-Mart was worth $2.5 million in January 2006. (How could we have missed that one?) The annual compounded rate was 28.2 percent.

- In August 2004, Google had its IPO. Stock opened at $85 and immediately jumped to $100 per share. In December 2005, it was trading at about $400 (an annualized increase of 307 percent).

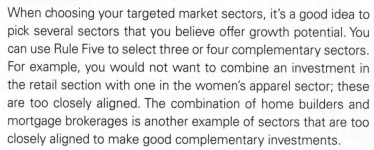

Applying Rule Five: Create a Complementary Combination of Investments

When choosing your targeted market sectors, it's a good idea to pick several sectors that you believe offer growth potential. You can use Rule Five to select three or four complementary sectors. For example, you would not want to combine an investment in the retail section with one in the women's apparel sector; these are too closely aligned. The combination of home builders and mortgage brokerages is another example of sectors that are too closely aligned to make good complementary investments.

Of course, predicting the hottest industry and then predicting the hottest company within that industry is a little like getting the stars to align. But let's give it a try. Even if we only get close a time or two, the results can be most gratifying.

"Let's talk about how to select which stocks we will buy," I say. "We begin by using stock selection filters to guide us as we make our choices." I pass out a list of the most popular stock selection filters. "As you look at the list, remember that no one uses all of the filters when selecting a trade."

Stock Selection Filters

Sales growth

Earnings growth and health

Product pipeline

Institutional investor activity

Stable or growing margin of profit

New offerings/buybacks

Activity spikes (volume)

Price volatility

Insider activity

Short-selling activity

Price-to-earnings ratio

Price-to-dividend ratio

The filters we list here appear in no particular order because their effectiveness changes with the market cycles. The filters that indicated the best results last year may not (likely, they will not) provide the best results this year. As a result, your use of these filters will, from time to time, need to be adjusted. Remember, you should not attempt to use every one of these filters.

"Hold on one moment. I've heard all these terms before, but I always thought they were called market indicators not market filters," says Lou.

"You're right," I respond. "Each one by itself can be an indicator providing us information about a company. However, you will see that as we use three or four indicators together, each will become a filter helping us narrow and refine our investment choices."

As a practical matter, successful investors choose to watch only a few filters and become proficient at their use. You likely will use three, four, or maybe five of the filters we discuss here when you make your stock selections. Again we need to remember Rule Two, "Invest, Succeed, Repeat," and Rule Seven, "Keep It Simple."

Using Proven Stock-Selection Filters

The majority of stock-selection filters are simple market indicators that offer straightforward information you can use to help guide your investment decisions. Let's take a look at those first.

Sales growth: One of the most basic indicators of a company's health is sales growth, so this is one of the more useful stock-selection filters. Because there are so many companies and so much data, it is a good idea to set minimum criteria for your search. For example, your ideal candidate might have experienced sales growth of 15 percent or greater for three consecutive years. You can do a simple search on an online investment site to find companies that fit this criterion. (Most online brokers offer search filters that will let you specify your criteria.)

Growth rate: Your investment style will help determine how much sales growth you look for when selecting a company's stock. At a 15 percent growth a company would double its size every five years. That is not a bad rate of growth. There are investors who are more aggressive and seek companies with annual growth rates of 50 percent or 75 percent. When making your choice, consider the growth rate of other companies in the same sector. If most companies in the sector are growing at 20 percent a year, then you probably want to avoid a company stuck at 15 percent.

Sustainability: You can, of course, find companies with 100 percent and 200 percent sales growth rates, but those rates are almost impossible to maintain. If your investment style is to be invested in the security for only a short time (a very acceptable style of investing), playing the hottest hand is a good idea. If you are a longer-term trader, you will want to invest in companies with a sustainable rate of growth.

Earnings health and direction: Great companies tend to show steady growth patterns with few surprises in their earnings history. Does the company's earnings history show a pattern of growth that makes sense? Earnings growth of 10 percent, 12 percent, and 10 percent over a three-year period, for example, is more appealing than a negative growth rate of 5 percent, followed by a positive growth of 35 percent, and then a year of zero growth. When working with this indicator, you also need to ask yourself if there is a reasonable expectation that earnings can continue to grow during your investment period. If a company's earnings rely on a product that is becoming obsolete, you might want to look elsewhere to invest your money.

New product pipeline: Growth rarely falls from the sky. Changes in a company's product line, services, or management are key indicators of future growth.

Institutional investor activity: You can learn a lot about a company's investment potential by checking this indicator. Who else likes this company? A check of a few financial Web sites will let you know if institutional investors such as mutual funds and banks are moving their funds into this stock.

Profit margins: Growing sales and shrinking margins don't cut it. Has there been unexplained erosion in margins? Growing sales with growing margins is a formula for riches.

New share offerings or stock buybacks: Has the company recently announced a secondary offering of additional shares? Such an announcement often has a bearish effect because it means that more shares will be available. Did the company start buying back some of its shares? Buybacks can have a positive effect for two reasons:

Fewer shares outstanding mean greater earnings per share.

The company's board believes that the stock is undervalued (*Barron's* reports on stock buyback activity every week).

Activity spikes: Spikes in trading activity can provide an important signal to investors. Stocks that advance (go up) on increased trading volume deserve attention, as do stocks that move downward on larger-than-usual volume. This information is available each day in *Investor's Business Daily* and on many online sites during the trading day.

Volatility: Stock volatility computations are available from many sources. Keeping an eye on stocks with increasing volatility (to the upside) can be a signal of increased investor interest in the company.

That takes care of some of the most basic market indicators. Now, let's talk about a few stock-selection filters that deserve a more detailed explanation.

Insider Trading Activity

Insider trading takes place when an insider (or a person controlled by an insider) trades in company stock using *material* information that is not available to the general public. Members of a company's board of directors, as well as its president, chief financial officer, and other officers are insiders. They have more information about the company, and they have a better view of the company's future than the general public. Just like any investor, company officers want to make good investments and bail out of weak investments. So it should be of interest to us if insiders are buying or selling stock in their company.

Trading by insiders is legal *if it is disclosed*. Regulations mandate that all insider trading be reported to the SEC by the close of business of the day following the transaction. Because insiders are required by regulation to disclose any transactions that they make in their company's stock, we can follow insider trading activity and use that information to our advantage when selecting stock investments.

Insider trading information is available in the press or from any of several online services. Historically, buying the stock of companies with strong insider buying and shorting companies with strong insider selling has produced better-than-average returns.

Short-Selling Opportunities

You may already know what short selling is, but just in case you don't, here's a one-minute explanation.

"Not so fast," says Anne. "I'll need more than a minute to understand this. I've heard the phrase 'selling short' many times, and the whole idea is a mystery to me."

"Okay, Anne," I say, "think of it this way. Every investor knows that stocks go in two directions: up and down. Even the healthiest stock zigzags on its route upward. If you see a stock that you believe will be going up, you should buy it, and if you see a stock that you think is going down, you should sell it."

"Sell it—what if I don't own it?" says Anne.

Let's say that you were looking at General Motors at $55. You believe that the stock is overpriced. You don't own any GM, but you still want to sell this dog. Not to worry. Simply call your broker (or log in to your online trading account) and place a sell order: "Hello, Mr. Broker, I want to 'sell short' 100 shares of GM." The broker sells the stock in your name. The broker will use GM stock he has in his inventory (likely another investor's GM stock) to complete the delivery. Your account reads as follows.

| Credit Cash | $5,500 (from the sale of 100 GM) |
| Debt Stock | 100 Shares of GM (that you need to pay back) |

Voilá! You were right; everyone loves the new Fords, and GM stock falls to $35 a share. To cover your short position, you buy 100 shares of GM at a cost of $3,500. Your broker uses the 100 shares that you have just bought to satisfy the debt balance in your account. Your account now reads:

| Cash | $2,000 |

That is short selling.

Short-selling activity data can be used as an indicator. When the number of short sales starts to increase as a percent of trading activity in a security, that stock is waving a flag saying, "Look at me." Short-selling activity is a signal to investigate further why some investors think this stock is about to decline. If you own the security, increased shorting activity may be the early signal to bail out of your position. If your investigation leads you to believe the people who are selling short are wrong, the increased shorting instead becomes your buy signal. If the stock goes up even a little, the shorts will need to cover their positions, creating a pool of future buy orders that will need to be filled.

How can you investigate the current short-selling activity of any stock? By SEC regulation, brokers must post this information. Several online services collect and organize short-selling activity into a usable format and make it available for a fee.

Price-to-Earnings and Price-to-Dividend Ratios

The price-to-earnings ratio, or P/E ratio, is the most basic of measures. This ratio is obtained by simply dividing a stock's price by its earnings per share. As a reference point, at the writing of this book, the 500 stocks in the S&P had an average P/E of about 17. The lowest average P/E ratio of the 500 stocks that make up the S&P was 6.1, back in 1950. The highest was a crazy 44.2, in 2001. Over the past fifty years, the P/E of the S&P 500 has averaged 17.5.

Here's how to use this indicator as a stock-selection filter. When comparing several stocks in the same industry, you may wish to look further at those stocks with a P/E ratio much higher or much lower than the others. Is the stock with the lowest P/E ratio a bargain? Or is it out of favor for a reason? The stock with the highest P/E ratio may be overpriced, or there could be a strong reason that investors believe that the company's future is exceptionally exciting. Consider this example, which compares five companies in the same industry.

Company	Stock Price	Annual Earnings per Share	P/E Ratio
V	$100	$5	20:1
W	$60	$5	12:1
X	$55	$5	11:1
Y	$50	$5	10:1
Z	$20	$5	4:1

In this example, both companies V and Z deserve extra investigation. Growth-stock investors may be intrigued with V and interested in why this stock is the "hot hand." Is there a promising new product on the horizon? Does the company have a lock on a key patent? Value-stock investors could be intrigued by company Z. They may believe it to be undervalued or even an undiscovered gem.

One note of caution: P/E ratios can become momentarily distorted by an abrupt event. President Eisenhower's heart attack in September 1955, the assassination attempt on President Reagan in March 1981, or the Dan Quayle spelling gaffe in June 1992 are examples of events that can jolt the market and throw P/E ratios into momentary disarray.

The P/E ratios for the 1,500 most widely held stocks are listed each day in the *Wall Street Journal*. You can also find this information in *Barron's* and *Investor's Business Daily* (IBD), as well as online.

IBD market listings also include the publication's own rating system of each stock. The IBD ranking is generally in line with what a growth-stock investor would be looking for.

On its own, a company's P/E ratio is not very meaningful. You need to evaluate it within the framework of the P/E ratios of other companies in the same sector. You can find this information by checking other stocks listed in the *Wall Street Journal* or online. Yahoo! provides a wealth of data, including industry P/E information, for free at *http://biz.yahoo. com/ic/*. Alternately, subscription services such as Standard & Poor's provide more supporting information than you could ever hope for.

Finally, many value investors like to use a stock's price-to-dividend ratio as a selection filter. These investors say, "Who cares how much the company says it's earning? I care about what it is willing to pay me in dividends."

In an awful imitation of Ricky Ricardo, Jack speaks up. "Lucy, you've got some 'splaining to do. What happened to 'Keep it simple'?"

"I know that the list of selection filters is long," I respond, "and they sound complex. However, remember you are only going to use a few of the filters, and the more you use them, the easier and more meaningful they will become."

Choosing the Filters That Fit Your Philosophy

The selection filters you decide to use are those that make sense within *your* market philosophy. You begin by using one selection filter. When you find the list of stocks that fits your first criteria, test that list against your second selection filter, then against the third filter.

With each successive filter, the field is narrowed until you have your investment candidate.

Of course, some investors just keep testing and testing, using a fifth, sixth, or seventh selection filter to obtain ever more confirmation. At some point, however, these folks can end up with analysis paralysis, unable to make an investment decision.

Which filter is best? It keeps changing. Each year it seems that a different filter is the "best" predictor. As an intelligent investor, you should use three or four selection filters. Let's go through the process of choosing a sector and then a stock within that sector:

Step one: *You have observed and read in the press that consumers are out shopping and spending like there's no tomorrow. Plus, you have learned from your broker's online Web site that there is a sector rotation into the retail sector (i.e., dollars flowing into retailing stocks).*

Action: *Look for stocks in the retail sector.*

Step two: *You choose the following stock-selection filters:*

Sales growth

Profit margin growth

Insider activity

Action: *Use an online site that allows you to progressively filter company data. (Your broker may offer a good filtering site at no charge.) After each progressive filter your list of investment candidates will be shorter and more manageable.*

List the stocks in the sector (in this example, retail).

Filter the list to select only the companies with improving sales.

Filter the list again to select only those companies with consistent or improving margins.

Finally, filter the list to select only the companies in that sector with increased insider buying.

Congratulations! You have your candidates.

Of course, you may not want to use the selection of filters we used in the example. Instead, you may decide that these are better indicators for you:

- New product pipeline

- Stock price volatility

- Increased trading volume

No matter which stock-selection filters you choose, *stock selection can and should be treated as an information-driven process.* The process requires a little work. No one rings a bell or flashes a blue light to tell you where to look for the next Microsoft or Wal-Mart. But the clues are out there just waiting to found.

How Warren Buffett Does It (You Can Do It, Too)

A discussion of investing that excluded Warren Buffet would be like a conversation about baseball that left out Babe Ruth and Willy Mays. Buffett's annual letters to shareholders are taught in MBA courses across the country. Amazon.com lists 135 books with his name in the title, and a Google search on his name returns more than two million hits. Why is Buffett so respected? Is it because he is the coolest guy in Nebraska and has a never-ending catalog of folksy things to say? No, it's because of his accomplishments as an investor.

One of my favorite Buffett remarks came when a reporter asked him how it felt to slip from number-one slot on the *Forbes* list of "The 400 Richest People in America" to number two, behind Bill Gates. Buffett replied, "I guess I could think about the one person who is ahead of me, or I could think about the 250 million who are behind me."

You will recall that earlier we talked about the work of Rex Sinquefield, who established that most investors, professional or amateur, do not perform as well as the S&P 500 market index. According to Sinquefield's data, the most a typical investor should hope for when investing over a forty-year period is to outperform the S&P about twenty times and underperform the S&P about twenty times. In a forty-year history of Buffett's investment company, Berkshire Hathaway (1964 to 2004), Buffett has outperformed the S&P thirty-six times.

To understand the impact of Buffett's superior trading, consider this. The annual compounded growth rate of the S&P during the period (assuming all dividends are reinvested) was 10.4 percent. At that rate, a $22,000 investment in the S&P on December 31, 1964, would have grown to a value of $1,169,960 on January 1, 2005—not bad.

Over the same period of time, Berkshire Hathaway's stock achieved an annual compounded return of 21.9 percent. At that rate of return, the same $22,000 investment on December 31, 1964, would have grown to be worth $63,110,299 on January 1, 2005. That's right: more than $63 million. The difference between Berkshire Hathaway's performance and that of the S&P over the same forty-year period is almost $62 million!

I selected the investment amount of $22,000 for this example because it represents a benchmark for our comparison. In 1964, the average price of a new home in America was $22,000. On January 1, 2005, the average home price was $223,000. Most Americans will say that home prices have skyrocketed since the mid-1960s, but when we compare the forty-year change in the value of our three hypothetical investments, we get a clearer picture.

Investment	1964 Value	2005 Value
Home	$22,000	$223,000
S&P	$22,000	$1,169,960
Berkshire Hathaway	$22,000	$63,110,299

"Now it's your turn," I say. "If you want to invest like Warren, please raise your hand." Everyone snickers a bit, and then all raise their hands.

"Okay," I tell them. "Here's his secret potion—get ready to rub it all over your body. *Buffett uses common sense when making his investment decisions.*"

Common sense, what a concept! You know the old saying, "Common sense isn't very common." Here are the elements of Buffett's method:

- Buffett is a value investor. He knows his investment philosophy, and he sticks with it. (See Investment Rules Two, Four, Seven, and Eight.)

- His selection filters tend to ignore the stock market and focus directly on the company. For Buffett, a filter such as sector rotation would not be meaningful.

- The first filter Buffett uses (okay, I don't really know the order, but it doesn't matter) is return on equity, abbreviated as ROE. This indicator answers the question, "Has the company historically provided a good return on equity for its investors?" ROE is generally a good indicator of how well a company is run by its management. To compute ROE you simply divide the total shareholder equity into the company's net income (net income/shareholder equity).

- Buffett also checks the company's debt-to-equity ratio, which indicates whether a company has used its debt judiciously. Buffett likes a low ratio because it means that future earnings can be reinvested in the company or paid out to shareholders, as opposed to being earmarked for debt repayment. This also gives the company freedom to act without the scrutiny of large creditors who second-guess every management decision.

- Good profit margins matter to Buffett, too, as they indicate that management is running a tight ship. Buffett also looks for the potential to increase margins. Is there something about the product that a consumer will pay an extra $.01 and still buy it in the same quantity?

- No start-ups for Buffett—he likes established companies. Sure, he'll miss out on opportunities like eBay and Google, but he'll also avoid the companies that burn bright and then flame out each year.

- Buffett also asks, "Is there something that keeps the product special?" He knows that commodity products that end up selling at thin margins are to be avoided.

- Most of all, Buffett wants to know if the investment is a value. Can its stock be bought at a price lower than the company's intrinsic value? For value investors such as Buffett, buying a stock for more than its intrinsic value is mere speculation. (For more information on intrinsic value, check out my Web site, at *www.dennisblitz.com*.)

- Finally, Buffett likes businesses that he understands. No nuclear-powered rocket-ship builders, no black box software encryption companies. Just good, clean businesses that anyone could talk about over the businessmen's special at lunchtime.

Buffett's use of the above criteria has lead Berkshire Hathaway to make investments in some very fine companies. Buffet doesn't trade stocks; he makes long-term investments in businesses that he feels comfortable sticking with. Here is just a partial list of Berkshire's investments:

GEICO Insurance	Controlling position
General Re Insurance	Controlling position
American Express	151 million shares
Coca-Cola	200 million shares
H&R Block	16 million shares
Moody's Corporation	24 million shares
The Washington Post	2 million shares
Wells Fargo & Company	53 million shares

Berkshire also holds major positions in Shaw Industries, Nebraska Furniture Mart, Borsheim's Jewelry, Benjamin Moore Paints and Coatings, Fruit of the Loom, Dexter (shoes), Kirby Vacuum Cleaners, See's Candies, The Pampered Chef, CORT (office furniture rental), Clayton Homes, Net Jet, and many others.

Is Warren Buffett doing anything that you cannot do yourself? Here is a suggestion. Think back to the description of Buffett's method, each time I used his name, insert your name instead. The point is that we can all do what Buffett does if we choose to.

In fact, it may be possible for you to outperform Buffett. He himself points out that the market capital of Berkshire is now so large that he needs "elephant deals" to move his result a single point. For the rest of us ordinary investors, a few simple intelligent investments will have a significant impact on your return.

1. Invest in what you know. When it comes to investing in the stock market, readers are leaders. Stay current. Read everything: *Barron's*, *BusinessWeek*, *Forbes*. The more rounded your knowledge of the business climate, the better you will do.

2. Invest, succeed, repeat. Over time, you will sort out the market filters that you find most reliable for you. Then use them again and again.

3. Embrace the learning curve. It takes a little time to select the filters that you like best.

4. Avoid losing money. Never make bet-the-house investments.

5. Complementary investing. Invest in industries that do not align.

6. Take charge of one investment. Do it yourself. You're just as smart as the money managers and a lot less expensive.

7. Keep it simple. You don't need to own every stock or use every selection filter.

8. Trust your method. Not every trade is a winner. It is the overall portfolio performance that counts in the end.

9. Rebalance your portfolio. When a stock goes up, don't be greedy; take your profits. Hitting a single ten out of every fifteen times at bat puts you in the Hall of Fame in Cooperstown.

Author's Note

This section on stock selection is based on a method of selection called fundamental analysis. There is another school of thought that suggests that technical analysis (a stock's price and volume history) can also provide guidance to the future price activity of a stock. While I do not suggest that technical analysis is superior to fundamental analysis, some people have found that a basic understanding of price and volume movement can be helpful. If you are interested in learning more about technical analysis, you can visit my Web site, where you will find a paper on the topic. Go to *www.dennisblitz.com* and click on "Book Supplement."

Finding Great Information Online

Earlier, I mentioned that with current technology and the Internet as a distribution channel, today's investors have more data at their fingertips than the most sophisticated investor of the 1970s or 1980s. Some online services make this information available free of charge, while others charge a subscription fee. I have divided the reviews that follow into those two categories.

Free Sites

Free sites offer a lot of very useful information. They generally require that you register with your name, e-mail address, and other basic information, so they can market their site to advertisers. When signing up for a free site, you should expect to get a steady stream of marketing offers—which I consider a small inconvenience when compared to the value of all the data the sites provide. Most advertisers are very responsive to removing your name from their marketing list if you simply ask to unsubscribe. Free sites also earn money by offering for-purchase analyst reports.

The following free sites offer a side range of data for any investor.

123 Jump IPO Center: www.123jump.com

Here, you'll find lots of articles on current business news. Most of the focus is on IPO activity, including commentary about upcoming offerings and a handy IPO calendar. The site also offers charts and a mutual-fund question-and-answer section.

Big Charts: www.bigcharts.com

As the name implies, this site offers excellent charts and graphs, along with some basic interactivity. You easily can call up other general information about a company while at a given chart. Of the free chart sites, this may be the best.

BusinessWeek Online: www.businessweek.com

As you might expect, this site is excellent for business articles. It's a bit weak, however, for direct stock picking.

CNNMoney: http://money.cnn.com

If you can't switch on CNBC for your market fix, this is a good page to check out. The stories are lively, quick reads. On the other hand, other sites offer more filters to help you make investment decisions. One superior feature on the CNNMoney site is that it tracks company earning estimates for the past ninety days and lists how many times the earning estimates have been revised.

Earnings.com: www.earnings.com

This site features live Webcasts and replays of earnings calls, annual meetings, and investor meetings. The site has an excellent events calendar that displays earnings dates, conference calls, and more.

Hoover's Online: www.hoovers.com/free

This site is loaded with in-depth information on 42,000 companies. IPO investors will like the "IPO's on Deck" section (at www.hoovers.com/global/ipoc), which contains data on almost every IPO, the filings, a calendar, a scorecard, and much more. Hoover's offers additional data for a fee.

Investopedia: www.investopedia.com

This is another good site for beginners. Tutorials, a glossary, and a respectable selection of articles are its strong points, but the stock filters and stock ideas sections are nothing to write home about.

IPO Home: www.ipohome.com

This is an easy-to-use site for anyone just starting out in the IPO arena. The site assumes that the reader is a newbie and offers a welcoming approach, along with many of the same types of data that can be found at the other IPO sites.

MarketWatch.com: www.marketwatch.com

This is a Dow Jones product. It's current, professional, and very well designed. The site has detailed balance sheets, income statements, and cash flow reports on thousands of companies, and it offers personal finance, newsletter and research, and investment filters sections. It has good data on insider buying and selling and a tracking feature that shows analyst recommendations for the past five years. The site also includes a listing of market analysts' upgrades and downgrades during the past five years for each stock.

MSN Money http://moneycentral.msn.com/home.asp

By going directly to this page, you can bypass all those wonderful MSN articles about Britney Spears's belly button or what Dr. Phil thinks of people who wear brown shoes. You may want to go directly to the stock investing section (at http://moneycentral.msn.com/investor/research/welcome.asp). This MSN site offers news stories, company reports, SEC filings, and recent news sorted by company, including key developments, a basic chart filter, stock ratings, and estimates of future earnings. The site has sections for analyst ratings, financial results, insider trading data, and both a simple and deluxe stock screener filter. In my opinion, the filters don't do a very good job of narrowing the field of investments. MSN also provides information on IPOs, a well-designed feature that clearly shows any "earnings surprise" that occurred over the past five quarters.

Reuters: www.investor.reuters.com

The most storied name in financial reporting offers a solid Web site, with sections for real time quotes, news, financial highlights, ETFs, options, commodities, and much more. I like the "Sentiment" section, which contains data on stock performance, shares shorted, insider trading, and each stock's institutional holdings. Reuters's institutional holdings section is among the best. The site also provides five years of cash-flow data on thousands of companies, plus an analysis section that offers risk alerts and recommendations.

ValuePro: www.valuepro.net

ValuePro computes a "theoretical value" for each stock based on twenty variables, including percent growth rate, working capital, short-term liability, and company stock Beta. The site has very good data on company cash-flow history. Plus, ValuePro allows you to play "what if" games right online. The value of a stock is based on several components. You can change any one of the component factors, and the site recalculates the stock's theoretical value.

Whisper Number: www.whispernumber.com

The filters on this site do a better-than-average job of trying to predict the next quarter's earnings. Whisper Number doesn't stick its neck out too far, though; it limits its predictions to the next quarter's results only.

Yahoo! Financial: http://finance.yahoo.com

The Yahoo! Financial site is similar to the MSN site, but it's worth visiting both. Beyond differences in page layout, the two sites have subtle differences in their features. When researching a stock on Yahoo!, for example, you can easily get data about the company's competition with just one click. Yahoo! also provides a list of institutions and mutual funds that hold each stock plus data on how much each holds. Like many sites, Yahoo! offers a free "stock alert" filter.

Zacks: www.zacks.com

This Chicago-based investment analysis company hit it big when Wall Street began to go outside for analysis services. Over the past three years, it has greatly upgraded its consumer Web site. The site offers a very nice portfolio tracking section, as well as a ranking section that is better than most. The "Zacks Number 1 Ranking List" is worth a visit, as are the research and stock screening filters.

There are hundreds of other free sites available. Some worth reviewing include these:

ADR.com: www.adr.com

American Stock Exchange: www.amex.com

Bloomberg.com: www.bloomberg.com

Bond Page: www.bondpage.com

Chicago Board of Options: www.cboe.com

Chicago Board of Trade: www.cbot.com

EFT Connect: www.etfconnect.com

Euroland: www.euroland.com

Investing in Bonds: www.investinginbonds.com

Invest in REITs: www.investinreits.com

Morgan Stanley: www.msci.com

REIT Net: www.reitnet.com

Russell: www.russell.com

Standard & Poor's: www.standardandpoors.com

Treasury Direct: www.treasurydirect.gov

Wilshire Associates: www.wilshire.com

Subscription Sites

You shouldn't let a subscription fee turn you away from a site. The information is a bargain when you consider the hours it would take you to do the research yourself. In general, subscription sites tend to offer more detail. Their charts and graphs can be manipulated to emphasize the information that you want to research, and the stock screening filters are more flexible. If you are going to make your own stock market investment decisions, I believe that the small cost of a subscription site is a good investment. Any subscription site can easily pay for itself many times over with just one good trade.

Here is a list of worthwhile subscription sites:

Dorsey Wright: www.dorseywright.com ($25/month)
If you are hooked on "point and figure" charts, this is nirvana.

MarketScreen.com: www.marketscreen.com ($30/month)
This site gives market calls based on both fundamental and technical input.

Morningstar: www.morningstar.com (variable, to $125/year)
This site provides comprehensive financial information on just about any stock or mutual fund available.

SmartMoney.com: www.smartmoney.com ($29.95/month)
This site provides a ton of free information, but paying the monthly fee gives you access to a more in-depth view and a very nice stock-screening filter.

StockCharts.Com: www.stockcharts.com ($20/month)
This site is chart heaven, offering enough free charts to keep most people happy. The monthly fee gives you access to even more.

General Information Sites

Here are some sites you may want to list on your favorites menu:

Bloomberg.com: www.bloomberg.com

Financial Planning Took Kit: www.finance.cch.com

Internal Revenue Service: www.irs.gov

NASD: www.nasd.com

Risk Grades: www.riskgrades.com

Social Security Online: www.ssa.gov

The Motley Fool: www.fool.com

10: Investing in Equity Options

"Options! Not for me. I've heard they're risky and that you need to be glued to your computer screen all day if you plan to trade these things," Tim barks.

"That can be true," I respond. "However, by using Rule Three, 'Embrace the Learning Curve,' we will easily overcome that misconception and make options a powerful profit tool for our portfolio."

Picture this: You have a well-balanced portfolio of investments. Your holdings include seven or eight stocks in companies that you believe are solid and worth owning. Each month, with as little as a few hours of work at your computer, you make a few simple options trades. As a result, you generate extra earnings from your stocks of 10 percent to 15 percent a year.

Or let's say that you have a large position in one stock, and you are seeking a way to protect yourself from a possible market decline. In addition, you want the protection at no cost to you.

Sound interesting? Welcome to options trading.

Trading options can be more (far more) speculative than trading stocks, or it can be more conservative. Options can give you the heart-stopping thrills of betting on a horse race, or they can be as boring as watching the grass grow. Your experience will be determined by the strategy you select.

Many people start out believing that trading in stock options is the way to make a big score, and yes, that can happen. Most successful option traders, however, do not "swing for the fence" each time they are at bat. Instead, they are patient people who enjoy working a strategy. To be a successful options trader, you must see the big picture. No single option trade is all that important. Options traders *know* that they will have losses. The successful options trader simply strives to have more winning transactions than losing ones and to have each win be a little bigger than each loss. The trader who takes the time to hone his knowledge and polish his skills will be richer for the effort.

As in any market, people who rush into options trading without a plan are likely to be disappointed with their results. The rudimentary strategies presented here have worked for thousands of investors.

Looking round, I sense some discomfort. Options are unknown territory to this group.

"I've never even considered options. I hope you plan to start at ground zero," says Lou.

"Okay, that's just what we will do," I say.

The Basics

"Options trading has its own language," I begin. "Before we begin discussing strategy, we need to understand a few basic definitions." Out of the corner of my eye, I see Mark taking copious notes, as usual. "The simple primer in options trading that follows," I continue, "will give you the foundation information you need to start developing your own method for successful investment in equity options."

Buying and Selling Call Options

When we buy call options, we are, in effect, paying for the opportunity to buy ("call") a stock by a future date at a preset price. The future date is when the option *expires*; the preset price is called the *strike price*. The buyer of the call option has a right to purchase the stock before the option expires at the strike price but is not obligated to make that purchase.

The amount the buyer of the call option pays for this privilege is called the *premium*. By accepting the premium, the seller accepts the risk that he may be called upon to sell the stock at the predetermined price.

Selling a call option is also referred to as *writing* a call option. The writer (seller) is obligated to sell the stock *if* the buyer of the option exercises his option to call (buy) the stock. Whether the option is called or not, the writer keeps the premium.

To streamline this discussion, we will focus on buying and selling (also called writing) call options rather than put options. The buyer of a *put* contract is buying the option to sell a stock at a predetermined price by a predetermined expiration date, with the premium going to the writer of the put. (See "Options as a Conservative Investment Tool," later in this chapter, for a discussion of how to use a put.)

The Strike Price

As we mentioned earlier, the strike price is the preset price at which an option can be exercised. Strike prices can be set at any level. To keep things simple, listed options are priced in a sequence of equal increments. Generally, the sequence is set at $2.50 per share, but the increments can be $5, $10, or $20, depending on the price of the underlying security. In the case of a stock costing $26 per share, increments will be $2.50. We can expect that listed options will be offered with strike prices of $20, $22.50, $25, and so on. For a call option, a strike price lower than the current per-share price is referred to as *in the money*. Strike prices higher than the current per-share price of a stock are referred to as *out of the money*.

Listed options expire on the Saturday following the third Friday of each month. Typically, options can be bought for time periods as far out into the future as nine months. A special class of options, called long-term equity anticipation securities (LEAPS), includes options that are written as far out as two and a half years.

Three variables come into play when setting option prices:

- The price of the underlying security: This is the per-share trading price of the stock. Let's say we are looking at options in Microsoft (MSFT), and MSFT is trading at $27.50. An option priced at $25 would be in the money, while one priced at $30 would be out of the money.

- Volatility: The volatility of the underlying stock is critical in pricing the option. A stock that has wide swings in its price will cause the options on that stock to trade at a higher premium.

- Time to maturity: The longer the time to maturity, the higher the premium. This makes perfect sense because a longer time period allows more time for price fluctuation of the underlying security. The change in premium is not directly proportional to the time to maturity. While the premium of a two-month option will be higher than that of a one-month option, it will not be double. A three-month option will be more expensive yet, but not triple the one-month premium.

Option Trading

Option trading changed significantly in the early 1970s. Before then, options were written as private contracts. Because of this, options trading was a practical tool for only the largest and most sophisticated investors. When the Chicago Board of Options Exchange (CBOE) opened for business on April 26, 1973, it provided a process for trading "listed" options in a uniform manner, the same way that the futures markets trade uniform contracts of commodities. The CBOE publicly posted all contract requirements, data, and prices.

On the first day, the CBOE traded about 900 contracts covering sixteen different securities. Today, there are actively listed options on about 3,600 underlying securities, as well as LEAPS contracts on about 850 securities. Trading volume can reach as many as 2 million option contracts traded per day. Private (off exchange) trading in options still goes on today, but it is confined to the custom needs of large portfolio holders such as insurance companies, which must protect their assets.

Seats on the new CBOE were offered for $17,500 in April 1973. In May 2007, a CBOE seat sold for $3.1 million. Didn't I realize that listed options would be a big thing? Sure I did! But in 1973 money was still tight for me. I needed tires for my Chevy Nova, and I was getting married in just a few months. Today, the Chevy is gone, and so is my first wife. Maybe I should have bought that CBOE seat.

Buying Options as a Speculative Investment

With the definitions out of the way, we're ready to talk strategy. Let's begin by making a few simple trades.

The simplest trade is to buy a call. You would consider this action if you believed that the price of a security was about to increase. In this example, we will use Apple Computer stock, with a market price of $64.44 a share. You believe that the stock will appreciate. You have three ways to invest in Apple:

1. Buy 100 shares of Apple at a cost of $6,466.

2. Buy 100 shares of Apple on margin (currently at 50 percent), at an out-of-pocket cost of $3,233, and carry a debit balance with your broker for the unpaid amount.

3. Buy a $65 one-month call option that will allow you to buy Apple for $65 at any time before the close of business on the third Friday of the following month.

In the real world, there are several strike prices and time periods that you may select depending on your goals. For now, however, let's just stick with the $65 one-month call option.

Assume that the premium for the one-month $65 call for Apple is $3.30. Since listed option contracts are for 100 shares of the underlying stock, the price of buying this call will be $330 for one contract.

"Wait a minute. I'm lost," says Lou. Lou is probably speaking for a few others who don't want to admit they're overwhelmed with the number of moving parts.

"Don't be concerned," I say "The feeling of being lost is only temporary." From behind my chair, I pull out a big pad of paper and a marker. "Here," I say. "I'll write out a little chart that may make it clearer."

Let's break down our investment choices.

Investment Scenarios

Type of Trade	Out-of-Pocket Investment (Plus Commissions)
Buy 100 Apple at $64.66	$6,466.00
Buy 100 Apple at 50 percent margin	$3,266 plus interest
Buy a one-month $65 call	$330

How would we earn a profit? Let's draw another table that shows the per-share price necessary for our investment to begin earning a profit given the three scenarios we've outlined. (The examples do not include the cost of commission.)

Profit Point

	Type of Trade	We will earn a profit if:
(The example does not include the cost of commission.)	Buy 100 Apple at $64.66	The stock increases in value beyond $64.66.
	Buy 100 Apple at 50 percent margin	The stock increases in value beyond $64.66 at a rate fast enough to offset the interest on the margin debt.
	Buy a one-month $65 call	The stock moves above $68.30 a share within the contract period. This amount equals the per-share strike price of $65.00, plus the $3.30 per-share premium cost.

Now, we need to consider the risk involved in this purchase. The next table shows just how much we might lose in each of the three scenarios. (The example does not include the cost of commission.)

Maximum Risk

Type of Trade	Ending Stock Price	Maximum Risk
Buy 100 Apple at $64.66	$0	$6,466
Buy 100 Apple at 50 percent margin	$0	$6,466 plus the interest on the margin loan
Buy one-month $65 call	$65 or less	$330

How would the profitability of these three investment strategies differ? The following table lists the gross returns (by both dollar amount and percentage) that will be achieved by each of the three scenarios if Apple reaches $72 a share before the option expires.

Gross Returns at $72

Type of Trade	Dollar Profit at $72	Percent Profit at $72
Buy 100 Apple at $64.66	$734	11.35%
Buy 100 Apple at 50 percent margin	$734 less the cost of interest	22.7% less the cost of interest
Buy one-month $65 call	$370 ($72 − $68.30 = $3.70 × 100 shares)	112% profit

Looking at the charts we just completed, Tim says, "Buying call options looks like a great idea."

"It sure looks that way," adds Lou.

"Well," I say, "it *is* a great idea . . . *if* the stock makes a major move up in a short time (as above). Let's run the same example, but this time let's say Apple remains unchanged at $64.66 a share through the expiration of the option." I pick up the marker again. "This chart tells the story."

Gross Returns with Unchanged Price

Type of Trade	Dollar Profit at $64.66	Percent Profit at $64.66
Buy 100 Apple at $64.66	$0	0%
Buy 100 Apple at 50 percent margin	Out the cost of margin interest	Out the percent of margin interest
Buy one-month $65 call	−$330	100 percent loss

As a matter of fact, the call-option buyer would have a 100 percent loss if the stock remains at or below $65 a share. At increases above $65 per share but lower than $68.30, the loss will be reduced. Only when the stock passes above $68.30 a share can the option trader expect to profit. From this exercise, you can see why many call contracts bought for speculation expire as "worthless."

At the core of the problem for speculators buying call options is the difficulty of overcoming the cost of the premium in a short time. Using the previous example, here are other choices we could make to address this difficulty:

1. Pay a lower premium. We can lower the one-month premium in this example to about $1.50 a share, if we buy a call with a higher strike price, such as $70 a share. However, the problem with this strategy is that to reduce the premium, the stock must reach a higher strike price to earn a profit.

2. Give it more time. We can buy a call that will provide more time for the stock price to advance. A three-month option will give a lot more time, but it will require a higher cost.

3. Select a stock with lower volatility. The lower a stock's volatility, the lower will be the premium cost of the option. Again, however, we can see a problem. The low volatility of the security means that the likelihood of significant price fluctuation is small.

"So with all of that," asks Anne, "why should we bother with options at all? It sounds as if there are problems no matter what we do with them."

"I don't want to be too negative regarding the use of options as a speculative investment tool," I reply. Options provide two significant advantages.

- A predefined and limited amount of risk: You can only lose the cost of the premium.

- Excellent leverage: With a small investment in a call option, you can control a large block of stock.

However, buying options to make a killing in the market is an unreliable strategy and for most investors is an investment that should be used very sparingly, if at all.

"Based on what you said earlier, I thought options were going to be a money machine," says Tim. "So far I don't see it."

"Hold your horses," I reply. "It may not be a money machine, but what comes next may warm your heart and your bank account."

Writing Options to Produce Regular Income

"This is it! Hold onto your chair! When you hear this next strategy, you may go running from the room yelling out loud, 'Where have you been all my life?'" Everyone laughs. "At least, that's the way this trading method is presented at option seminars."

I have watched many presentations on this next trading technique, and each time it is delivered as if the speaker had just found the Holy Grail. I don't know that I would go that far, myself. I will, however, share with you the information you need to make a profit using this technique. I'll also give you a heads-up about some of the dangers you will need to avoid along the way.

The Magic of the Covered Call

Okay, it's not really magic.

Writing a covered call is a simple two-step process:

1. You already own or you buy a security. In this example, you buy 100 shares of IBM stock at the market price of $83.10 a share. This is your "underlying security."

2. You sell to open, meaning that you sell (write) a one-month call option on IBM at $85. Because you are the writer, you do not pay the premium, you receive it. The premium for this option is about $.80 a share. Because a listed contract is always for 100 shares, you earn premium income of $80 for the contract. (There will be commission costs.)

After you have written this covered call, two things could happen:

1. The option expires with IBM stock at $85 or less.

2. Before the option expires, the price of IBM stock rises above $85.

Let's compare the result:

1. The option expires with the stock at $85 or less. In this case, the stock will not be called. You (the writer of the option) keep the premium, and you still own the stock. Your return is 0.96 percent (the amount of your premium income, $80 ($.80 X 100) divided by your investment $8310.00 ($83.10 X 100). This is almost a 1 percent return in only one month. You can simply put the premium income in your pocket and think of it as a bonus dividend. Or you can think of the premium income as reducing

your cost basis in the stock. In any case, as the owner of the stock, you can now repeat the process again with the same stock next month.

2. Before the option expires, the stock rises above $85. In this case, the stock will be "called." The person who bought the call option will want your stock, and will pay you $85 for it. In addition to earning a profit of $1.90 a share ($85.00 − $83.10), you keep the premium ($.80 per share). Your return will be: $1.90 + $.80 = $2.70 a share (3.2 percent in one month). Once the stock is "called away," it's gone and you are out of the game. If you want to write (sell) a covered option in IBM next month, you will need to buy new IBM stock for your portfolio.

In the above example, you could earn a higher premium by writing a longer-term option. A two-month option will sell for a higher premium (although, as we mentioned earlier, not for twice the premium of a one-month option).

Comparing Call Options with Different Strike Prices

Let's look at another example of writing call options. This time you will try ExxonMobil (XOM) trading at $61.20 a share. In this example, we will compare two different strike prices:

1. Buy 100 ExxonMobil at the market $61.20 and immediately write a one-month call for ExxonMobil with a strike price of $62.50.

2. Buy 100 ExxonMobil at the market $61.20 and immediately write a one-month call for ExxonMobil with a strike price of at $65.

The following table shows the results of these two strike prices both using one-month calls.

Comparison of Different Strike Prices

Strike Price	Premium Income	Premium Income as % of Investment	Earnings If Not Called	Earnings If Called
$62.50	$60	.0098	$60	$1.90 (3.1%)
$65.00	$15	.0025	$15	$3.95 (6.5%)

No doubt, having the stock called on a $65 option creates a much greater gain; 6.5 percent in one month isn't bad. However, the likelihood of the stock's rising to $65 is much less than the possibility that it will rise to $62.50. That is why you earn a much lower premium on the $65 strike price.

By changing the strike price, contract length, and premium, you can try a number of different combinations for writing call options. Different investors write covered-call options based on different strategies. Some gravitate toward using shorter (near-month) expiration options, while others like the higher premiums they earn from writing longer expirations. The examples used so far have been out-of-the-money options, but some investors like to write in-the-money options. Each combination presents a slightly different potential and risk/reward profile.

The fundamental point is that if you own a stock, you can write a call option, and you earn premium income. You can do this over and over, until you get tired of doing it or the stock is called. There are people who have been writing call options on the same stock for years by simply moving their strike price up and down in response to market conditions.

The Four Keys to Successful Covered-Call Writing

The idea of generating income from an otherwise idle asset is so appealing that several years back, some mutual funds started to write call options on much of their portfolios. What happened next should not have come as a surprise. The market had a few rallies, and the mutual funds that had written call options had much of their portfolio called away. Sure, the mutual funds earned premium income plus the appreciation when they sold the stock at the call price. At the same time, however, they missed the upside that came after the stocks were called, thus missing the lion's portion of the market move.

At this point Tim breaks in. "If I can earn a steady monthly premium on my stock plus a bonus pop of income if the stock gets called, it would be worth it for me to give up a 'big move' in a rising market." "Tim, I find no fault with that line of thinking," I say.

You do need to be careful of one important factor, however, and that is your selection of the underlying security. From reading the examples we've presented here, you might get the idea that you can buy any old stock, write call options, then just sit back and collect premiums. Not so. Remember that the largest component in your holding is the value of the underlying security, and no one wants the value of his or her largest component to decrease. If the underlying stock goes up in value, it is good news. However, if the underlying stock you selected suffers a significant loss in value, the income from premiums simply cannot make up for the decline in market value.

Here are some tips for selecting underlying securities:

1. Select underlying stocks that you believe (based on research using the stock selection filters) are solid and will remain stable in price, or better yet, will appreciate.

2. Be disciplined.

3. Be a steady player.

4. Understand that no single trade will make you rich. It is your ongoing monthly consistency that makes this process work in the long term. (There are no home runs, but there are a lot of solid singles.)

Options as a Conservative Investment Tool

So far, options have been discussed as a speculative tool and as an income-producing tool. The discussion now focuses on ways to use options as a conservative investment income tool.

Here's an example. Mr. Smith just sold his big idea to publicly traded General Dynamics Corporation (stock symbol GD). He was paid 10,000 shares of GD restricted stock. The restriction on the stock is that he may not sell the shares for one year. Now, Smith has a dilemma. He is satisfied with the price he received, and he likes GD as an investment in his portfolio. However, having too much committed to one stock is not prudent. What should Mr. Smith do?

Buying Protective "Puts"

For some investors, the answer to this question is simple. Mr. Smith can buy a *protective put* to cover the number of shares that he would like to protect.

The person who buys a put option has bought the right to put (sell) the underlying stock to the writer during the period of the contract at the strike price stated in the contract.

In our example, Smith owns 10,000 shares of GD Stock. The stock is currently trading at $64 a share. As this $640,000 is important to Smith, he wants to protect its value. To guard his value, Smith could buy a put. For example, if Smith buys a twelve-month put with a strike price of $62.50, no matter how far GD's stock price may fall, Smith can sell his stock to the writer of the put at $62.50. Smith's largest potential risk, in this example, is only a $1.50 a share (the difference between the current trading price and the strike price). In addition, if the stock remains unchanged, or even goes up in value, Smith will still own the stock and have the benefit from the appreciation. Sounds like a great idea, doesn't it?

Ah, but there is one little problem—the cost of the premium. In this example, the cost of the premium to protect against the stock declining below $62.50 for twelve whole months will be a whopping $14.10 a share. That is 22 percent of the value of the whole investment. As you can imagine, though the idea of having downside protection while retaining upside potential is very appealing, due to the high premium cost, few people seek to protect their portfolio in this manner.

The Collar Spread

But wait. What if you could get someone else to pay the premium for you? Sound interesting? The option-trading approach explained here is called a *collar spread*, and it is a conservative strategy.

To illustrate how a collar spread functions, let's keep working with those 10,000 shares of GD Corporation, trading at $64. Remember, your goal is to protect your position against a major loss for the coming twelve months. However, you want that protection at the lowest cost (or, better yet, at no cost).

Action	Collar Spread	Potential risk or reward	Cost or Income
We buy	A protective "put" for twelve months with a strike of $62.50	Maximum risk $1.50 per share	Cost $141,000
We write (sell)	A "call" for twelve months with a strike price of $67.50	Maximum profit $3.50 a share	Earning $145,000

Hence you have placed a "collar" around your position. At this point, there are only three things that could happen. The stock can go up, go down, or stay the same.

- If the stock falls below $62.50, the maximum you could lose is $1.50 a share.

- If the stock rises above $67.50, the maximum you could earn is $3.50 a share.

- If the stock remains between the two strike prices ($62.50 and $67.50), both options will expire without being exercised. You will keep the $4,000 profit from the two premiums, and you still own the stock.

Bob interrupts me. "So, simply stated, when we place a collar spread, we are giving up the opportunity to hit a home run in exchange for protection against a major downside move."

"Absolutely right," I respond. "Collar spreads are written every day by individuals, companies, and even governments interested in protecting their position and willing to give up some upside potential to have downside protection at virtually no cost.

"Would you like a larger upside potential than the one possible in the above example? No problem—just 'loosen your collar.' Buy a $60 put, and write a $70 call. The premiums will likely still offset each other. Sure, the upside potential is greater ($6 a share), but so is the downside risk ($4 a share)."

Tim steps in. "That's it, you lost me. Bob may understand this, but I'm having a difficult time Wasn't there an old country-western song called 'I'm My Own Grandpa'? This discussion of options is beginning to remind me of that song."

"Okay, maybe we should cut the topic of options trading here and call it a night," I say to the room.

"Not so fast," says Lou. "I'm really beginning to see the earnings potential that comes with the flexibility that options can offer. Let's keep going with this topic just a little more."

Using Option Straddles to Benefit from a Volatile Market

Collar spreads are an example of a combination options trade. There are many other examples of such trades, including *long straddles*.

Here's an example of the long straddle. You are sitting at home watching the news. Buried in the business section of the show is a story that goes like this.

"Tomorrow, the U.S. Supreme Court will hand down its verdict in the multibillion-dollar law suit of *Jones vs. Esquire Cruise Lines*. It seems that Jones went on a cruise and gained six pounds in one week because he stuffed himself at the midnight buffet every night. He is now suing the cruise line for $10 billion, claiming no one thinks that he is cute as a fatty."

From this story, you surmise two things:

1. Jones is a nut case, and maybe he should eat less.

2. The verdict could cause a significant impact on the price of the company's stock.

Even though you believe there will be volatility in the stock price, until the court announces its verdict, you don't know in which direction the stock price will move. How can you capitalize on the potential move in the stock price? By using a long straddle trade.

Esquire Cruise Lines stock is trading at $47.50 a share. You think that the stock price will jump in one direction or the other after the verdict is announced and that the movement in price will be substantial. You might buy one put with a strike price of $47.50 (current market price of the put $1.05 a share). You can use one month, called the *near month*, as your time to expiration; this will have the lowest premium cost, and you expect that the verdict and the resulting price fluctuation is going to happen very soon.

Simultaneously, you buy a near-month call for $47.50 (current market price $1.30 a share). Your total cost to buy the put and the call is $2.35 a share.

Let's restate your position:

- You currently own none of the stock.

- The stock is now trading at $47.50.

- You have a call that for one month allows you to buy the stock for $47.50.

- You have a put that for one month allows you to sell the stock for $47.50.

- Your cost so far has been $2.35 a share.

Now you sit back and wait until the court announces its verdict. There are two possible outcomes:

Jones gets nothing. The cruise line didn't make Jones eat the seven slices of chocolate cake each night. The stock rallies to $60 a share. You exercise your call option, buying the stock at $47.50 and earning a profit of $12.50 (less your costs of $2.35), and you are happy. (Don't forget to sell the now almost worthless put to get it out of your portfolio.)

Jones gets $10 billion. The cruise line is responsible for everything that happens on its ships, and the fact that Jones is no longer "cute" must be their fault. The stock plummets to $35 a share. You exercise your put, selling the stock at $47.50 and earning $12.50 (less your $2.35 cost), and you are happy. (Again, don't forget to close out the call.)

Sounds like a neat trade, so what can go wrong? Well, the volatility may not happen. If the stock remains flat, neither of the options will have value, and you are out $2.35 a share. Even if the stock moves just a little, there would still be a loss. Remember, to cover the costs of the trade (using this example), the stock would need to move above $49.85 or below $45.15 before the trader would realize a profit.

Writing an Iron Butterfly Spread

Let's do just one more spread, one called an *iron butterfly*. (I am using this type of trade as the next example primarily because I think the name is really cool.)

In the preceding example, you used a long straddle options strategy because you believed that the stock was going to be volatile. An iron butterfly spread can be used when you think that the stock you are observing is destined to go nowhere—in other words, you believe it's going to remain relatively flat.

One word of caution: When placing an iron butterfly, it's best that you own the underlying stock. Owning the stock is not a requirement, but it makes the trade safer because you may be required to deliver the stock if the stock price moves beyond its strike price(s).

An iron butterfly strategy would have been a fine choice to use with Wal-Mart stock for most of 2004 and 2005. The stock was stuck in a tight trading range, rarely trading above $50 or below $44. Let's say we place a trade, using Wal-Mart stock as our example. Assume that Wal-Mart (WMT) is at $48 a share. In this example, we write (sell) a one-month call with a strike price of $50 (premium received, $.55 a share). At the same time, we write (sell) a one-month put with a strike price of $45 (premium received $.30 a share).

Let's restate our position:

- We have received two premiums (because we wrote both the put and the call). Total premium received is $.85 a share. The $85 is our income. (An options contract is 100 shares of the underlying stock, so in this case it is $.85 × 100 = $85.)

- If Wal-Mart stock remains flat, neither moving above $50 or below $45, both options expire worthless, and we keep the premium income.

What can go wrong? If Wal-Mart stock moves either above $50 or below $45, we must cover the option. "Can you give an example of what would happen if the stock moves outside the range; for example, if the stock moves outside the range of $45 to $50 a share?" asks Lou.

"Sure. Let's say Wal-Mart stock goes to $53 a share. You would be required to sell 100 shares at the strike price of $50, thus realizing $300 less than you could have if you had not written the option. Conversely, if Wal-Mart stock dropped to only $41 a share, you would be obligated to buy it from the seller at $45, or $4 higher than the prevailing market value," I respond.

"So, an iron butterfly spread involves more risk than, say, writing a covered call," says Bob.

"Yes, that's right. You are really getting this," I say. "Butterfly spreads are great trades when written on a stock with a flat market price, but you accept a risk when you earn two premiums on a single trade."

Understanding Your Endless Options

The examples I have just presented have only scratched the surface of options trading.

- You can trade options at multiple prices.

- You can trade options over various lengths of time.

- You can trade options by either buying or selling them.

- You can combine any of these variables in combination trades.

With so much flexibility, the combination strategies when trading options are endless. An experienced options broker can construct a strategy for almost any investment situation.

Bob speaks up. "You know, this is very meaningful to me. I have several stocks in my portfolio that are just sitting there. Using options, I could be writing covered calls and picking up premium dollars. I also have a large position in the stock of my employer. I want to hold it, but I am concerned that if there were a sell-off, I could be slaughtered. So I want to look into the protection that options might offer."

"Bob is right," I say. "The important idea to take away from this discussion is that options open up ways to earn profits and to conserve the assets we already own."

Let's summarize how the Nine Rules of Successful Investing fit into option trading:

1. Invest in what you know. There are excellent books about this, and the CBOE Web site is filled with information that can help you start trading options.

2. Invest, succeed, repeat. If you write covered calls, repetition is one of the keys to long-term success.

3. Embrace the learning curve. The first few option trades may seem uncomfortable, but keep at it. The rewards can be very gratifying.

4. Avoid losing money. Options offer many "protective" strategies.

5. Create a complementary combination of investments. Options are a unique class of investments and are a good counterbalance to several types of investments.

6. Take charge of one investment. You can manage your strategy yourself.

7. Keep it simple. Select only one or two strategies and use them over and over.

8. Trust your method. No single option trade means the whole ball game. It is the results of your total trading activity that counts in the end.

9. Rebalance your portfolio. Just like anything else, your options trading may outperform (or underperform) your other investment groups.

However, remember this: *options are fairly priced*. In other words, the buyer of an option and the writer of the same option have an equal chance of being on the right side of the trade. Unless you are consistently better prepared than the other guy, options can turn into a neutral game, minus the cost of commissions.

If you want to learn more about options trading, the CBOE Web site (*www.cboe.com*) is a good place to begin. The site is loaded with free information, including tutorials, courses, seminars, and events.

Jack looks at his watch. "It's 11:00, and my head is swimming. I'm ready to call it a night."

Everyone agrees. "Let me make a suggestion," I say. "How about if each of us makes a stock trade using the filter method we talked about and maybe write a covered call before we get together next month. See you all right back here in July."

11: Fixed-Income Investments

A Little Safety Goes a Long Way

The last Saturday of July is a beautiful day. Some spend it on the golf course. Tim and Mark rent a fishing boat. I stay back at the cottage with a book and plans to take a long nap on the hammock. Jack is the only busy one. By early afternoon, he puts on an oversized apron and pulls every pot we have out of the cupboard. Tonight's dinner is his responsibility, and he is not going to let us down. At 6 p.m., the kitchen looks like a scene from a Godfather movie. Pasta, meatballs, veal, and several bottles of wine. The dinner lingers to almost 9:00. When it is over, we are all very full and in a very good mood. Even Bob has to admit that it was worth going off his Weight Watcher's regimen for the outstanding cuisine.

"How's that diet going?" Mark asks Bob.

"Well, not too good. So far I missed my first few meetings, and now this dinner. But I am really going to get started next week."

Mark rolls his eyes, and everyone tells Bob that they are sure that next week is the week. Bob tries not to be obvious as he lets his belt out a notch.

With dinner behind us, we settle down on the porch. By this time, the process is beginning to develop its own rhythm, and in a matter of minutes we are ready to begin. As I get ready to start, Tim (I think fortified by the wine) decides to question the evening's topic.

"I know that tonight we plan to talk about fixed investments, but come on! Do we really want to retreat to the safety of bonds? Why, that's not very macho is it! We need to take some risks if we hope to succeed. Didn't George Washington take risks at Valley Forge? Didn't Eisenhower take risks on D-Day? Didn't Rocky take risks getting in the ring with Apollo Creed?"

"That's true," I respond. "However, awe-inspiring as your examples are, when investing, let's remember Rule Four, 'Avoid Losing Money.'"

Another rule that applies to investing some of your assets in fixed-return assets is Rule Five, "Create a Complementary Combination of Investments." If you plan to make high-risk investments, it is wise to counterbalance your risks with the safety of fixed investments.

Balancing Your Risks

Sure, risk is necessary. Some risk is even fun. Everyone knows that if you bet $20 on a football game, you feel a heightened level of interest in the outcome of the game. When it comes to investments, however, you have to balance the enticement of a potential profit with the risk of a loss.

Think about it. If you make a good investment you may earn 10 percent, 15 percent, or even 20 percent. If you make a bad investment, you could lose 100 percent. Earning 15 to 20 percent can be difficult, yet losing it all is amazingly easy. Remember that it takes a lot of good investments to make up for even one stinker. Yet if we visit our local bookstore, we find shelves filled with books that promote only risk investments, titles such as *How to Make Money in Real Estate, How to Make Money in the Stock Market, How to Make Money in Foreign Currency Swaps.* Where are the books with titles like *How to Love T-Bills?*

Let me tell you how I learned the dangers of unbalanced risk. In 1982, the Environmental Protection Agency (EPA) approved a set of guidelines for a new testing method to be used on automotive catalytic converters. (The catalytic converter is a critical part in the emissions control system of an automobile.) If the converter passed the EPA test, it could be used as a replacement part on autos and trucks.

Around this time, an automotive engineer approached me with the idea of starting a company to buy, test, and certify used converters to be installed as replacement parts on cars and trucks whose converters had failed. He said that he knew how to build the testing equipment that would meet the new EPA standards. This engineer also suggested that he knew that the larger aftermarket manufacturers weren't interested in the product because the testing process didn't lend itself to high-speed production. If I put up the money, he reasoned, we could be more than just the first to the market—we would have the whole market to ourselves. "We could clean up," he said.

You have to understand that I know nothing about the auto aftermarket business, so I already was in violation of Rule One, "Invest in What You Know." But I was young and naive. I had just sold a business and was looking for an investment. What was to come next was out of a textbook of foolhardy moves. I had managed to walk headlong into the perfect set of circumstances to separate a man from his money. Let's look at the facts:

I had some money.

I was looking for a place to put it.

I was about to invest in an industry that I knew nothing about.

I considered the earnings potential of the investment without first considering the risk of the investment.

Recipe for Disaster

The idea looked great on paper. I could stop earning my living writing $25 books for aspiring stockbrokers and financial advisors. I would be in the business of producing $200 automotive aftermarket parts in a world where many of the over 475 million motor vehicles needed those parts. What an opportunity!

To keep this painful story brief, I invested (I will not say the amount because it hurts too much), and the partner turned out to be dead wrong. Several of the largest auto aftermarket manufactures *did* develop a similar product and were in the market only nine months behind us. The large manufacturers had both deep pockets and established distribution channels. Thirty-six months later, I sold the business at a 95 percent loss.

Moral: In investments, things can go wrong. Stocks can go down, bubbles can burst, real estate can sit unsold for months or even years, and competition can kill your product. Risk is real, and a portfolio without a portion in safe fixed investments is a risk that isn't worth taking.

T-Bills: The Do-It-Yourself Safety Net

U.S. Treasury bills (T-bills) are the gold standard of safe investments. Many fixed investments pay a higher rate of return, yet qualities such as the following make T-bills popular investments:

- Highest safety
- Very liquid and active market

- Almost no minimum or maximum investment limits

- Very low or even no-cost entry (commission-free)

- No management costs

Let's say that you have just received a large sum of cash. However, you do not yet have your long-term investment plan in place. Until you are ready, you need a safe, low-cost place to park the money. T-bills are an excellent choice. Or, if you are holding money for another person and are seeking safety, T-bills are ideal.

Buying a T-bill is a snap. They are issued in $1,000 denominations. Let your broker know how much you want to invest, and he will take care of the rest. Of course, you'll pay a commission. Better yet, you can walk into your bank and instruct them to buy T-Bills on your behalf. Depending on your relationship with the bank, they will charge very little for this service and in some cases nothing at all.

The best way to buy T-bills is directly through the U.S. Treasury. You have total control and pay no fees or commissions. Simply go to the U.S. Treasury Department Web site (at *www.ustreas.gov*), click on "Treasury Direct," then click "Open an Account." Complete the information requested.

Once you have completed the information, you make a bid. The only type of bid accepted on the site is called a noncompetitive bid. With this, you simply agree to accept the discount rate that is determined by the auction. (There is another type of bid called a competitive bid. With a competitive bid, you state the specific discount rate that you are seeking. However, this type of order must be entered through a bank or broker, and there is no guarantee that it will be filled.)

To make the noncompetitive bid, click the "Buy Direct" tab on the My Account page. Select what you want to buy (in this case, T-bills). Enter the amount you want to purchase and a purchase date. Answer the next few questions, and you are done. On the appropriate day, the U.S. Treasury Department will draw the correct amount of money from your checking account, and your account will be credited with the T-bills. The site even allows you to check a box to activate a rollover provision. Choosing this option is a good idea if you are not sure how long you will be using T-bills as your investment vehicle, and you want to be sure that your money is never idle.

Using CDs and Money Market Funds as Safe Havens

Some people leave short-term money in checking accounts or money market funds. If you leave large balances in your checking account, stop doing that now. Sure, the bank will love you for it, and balances that are left in checking accounts may earn some interest. However, the interest rates on these accounts can be as much as 300 basis points (100 bases points equals 1 percentage point) below the T-bill rate.

Another short-term option is a money market fund. Money market funds are great. They are liquid, you can invest any amount, and the management fees are very low. For the past few years, however, money market funds have paid less than T-bills—as much as 125 basis points less.

How about CDs? Bank CD rates tend to shadow the treasury rates. However, CDs have a holding period and charge a penalty for early liquidation.

In short, I cannot think of a situation in which I would recommend investing in a CD or money market fund over T-bills.

Investing in Corporate Bonds and Bond Funds

Interested in making longer-term investments? You might consider loaning your money to a company or a municipality. Municipal bond terms can extend thirty, fifty, and even ninety-nine years.

When buying a corporate or municipal bond, the first thing to look for is the bond's debt "rating," such as triple A, B, or C. The rating is a measurement of the bond issuer's probability of defaulting. The higher the rating, the more secure the bond's safety. The two largest bond-rating services are S&P Credit Service and Fitch Credit Ratings. Both use a similar scale. Below is the scale for Fitch.

- AAA: Highest Rating
- AA: Very Strong
- A: Strong

- BBB: Adequate

- BB: Uncertain

- B: Vulnerable

- C: High Risk

- D: Default or Liquidation

Bonds rated BBB or higher are referred to as *investment grade* bonds. This distinction is important because many fiduciary agreements are written with the provision that the money be invested in "investment grade bonds." Consequently, if a company's bond rating falls below BBB, the company's interest cost will be significantly higher, as fewer investors will be interested in buying their debt.

Beyond its rating, you need to consider a few other things when buying a corporate bond. First, the highest-rated corporate bonds pay only a small interest premium (commonly about 0.6 percent) over treasury debt with similar maturity. Next, you will pay either a commission or a spread to your broker to buy corporate bonds. To achieve a greater return from a corporate bond, you need to accept greater risk.

Extra Earnings, Extra Risk

Can you earn more from fixed investments? It's up to you. There are ample ways to increase the interest rate you earn on your fixed investment, but some of them require extra risk and extra work. Here goes:

1. Buy non-investment grade bonds (commonly called junk bonds). The name may be a bit ugly, but if you select your bonds carefully, you can earn a premium interest return.

2. Beat the bank on small-business loans. Banks price their business loans based on their cost of funds. A simple rule of thumb is that banks like to make business loans at a rate that is at least 2.75 percent to 3 percent higher than the current one-year CD rate they are paying to depositors. In your community, there may be many credit-worthy businesses that are seeking to borrow money and would be happy to split the difference with you. They might, for example, pay you 1.5 percent to 2 percent

more than the current CD rate and save themselves 1.5 percent to 2 percent in the process. Of course, you will want to have adequate collateral and a bottle of Sominex to help you sleep at night.

3. Loan money to real estate junkies. Every city has a long list of wannabe real estate developers. In some cases, banks are reluctant to deal with this group. (Maybe that should be a signal to you not to loan to them, either.) These borrowers, however, frequently come to the deal with good collateral (at the very least, the property they want to develop), and they are often willing to pay interest considerably over the prime rate—as much at 3 percent over prime is not uncommon. Thus, letting it be known that you are willing to consider making loans to real estate developers could bring a line of qualified buyers to your door.

Before You Make That Loan . . .

If you are considering making loans to businesses or developers, here are a few rules to follow:

1. Make sure you are dealing with someone who has successfully completed at least a few development projects or, in the case of a business loan, be sure the business is at least five years old and is cash-positive.

2. Ask to see at least two years of tax returns.

3. If the loan is guaranteed by real estate, either hold the title or, at the very least, record the loan at the county clerk's office. By recording your lien on the property, you are letting the world know that you must be paid before the property can be sold.

4. You may want to seek additional collateral, such as a second mortgage on the person's home.

5. Run a background check on the developer or businessperson. Check for a history of lawsuits, litigation, outstanding liens, or any involvement in a criminal proceeding. You can hire a local investigator to take care of this check, or you can use software to run the background check yourself. (Do an online search on the term "background-check software" to find some of the available

products.) These services are not expensive and are well worth their time and cost.

6. Ask an attorney to draw up the loan document and help you record your lien.

One last thing: If you are considering a business loan, carefully review the person's business plan. If the business plan looks ridiculous to you, walk away. No matter how much collateral you are holding, what you really want is to be paid back in dollars. The businessperson who wants to open up the city's largest combination fudge and sauerkraut stand or the developer who wants to build $900,000 homes in a neighborhood where the average home price is $270,000 may be nice guys, but I wouldn't loan them my money.

"Would you really make a loan to an individual?" asks Anne.

"Yes, I have made individual loans a number of times, and they have worked out well. I have a few criteria that I stick to, and that process has been successful," I respond.

"What type of criteria?" asks Bob.

"Tell you what—I will write out my list, and we can review it next month when we talk about real estate investing," I reply.

Finding Your Balance

All of us make our way through life deciding which risks we are willing to take and which we are better off avoiding. Investing is no different. As has been stressed before, every investment has some risk, and every investor should expect to make some mistakes. However a major investment mistake can be fatal to your financial health and recovering from a major setback can take years. That is why all investors need a safety net to counterbalance the necessary risks they accept as they put together their investment portfolio. Conservative investments such as T-bills and bonds aren't sexy investments, but they can help you sleep easier at night during times when your other investments are struggling. Of course, if you're lying awake at night thinking about the future, you may decide that you want even more strength in your safety net. If so, Chapter 12 discusses annuity contracts.

Just as I get ready to move to the next topic, Tim stops me. "I see the point of having a safety net, but doesn't having bonds in your portfolio by definition restrict your return?"

"Not really," I say. "In the long term, a portfolio with a portion of its assets in fixed investments can outperform one with no fixed-return investments. (Remember the discussion in Chapter 4 of Harry Markowitz, Nobel Prize winner, and his eighty-twenty rule?). Not only does having some fixed-return investments cushion our portfolio when the rest of the market is going south, they also allow us to take a few more risks with some of our dollars. I'm not a Nobel Prize winner, but if you ask me, having some of your money in fixed return investments is like chicken soup; it can't hurt."

12: Annuities

Peace of Mind at a Price

Mark is the first to bring up the obvious point: "You must be kidding. I've never heard anyone suggest that insurance is an investment." "True," I say, "but even though you may not immediately make that connection, the insurance industry has stepped in to provide investment-type products."

If you consider an investment to be a situation in which you place your funds in an asset with the intention that you or your heirs will receive a greater amount of money in the future, then many insurance products fit that description. Moreover, if you look at a variable annuity contract, you find that it is clearly an "investment contract," using a 1946 U.S. Supreme Court definition that a security is a "contract whereby the earnings depend solely on the efforts of a promoter or third party" (*Securities and Exchange Commission v. W.J. Howey Co.*, 328 U.S. 292 [1946]).

So, when referring to insurance company products as *investments*, our focus will be on annuities. For our purposes, the interesting thing about annuities is that during the annuity accumulation period (the time when you are putting money into the annuity), there is an interface with Rule Six.

Carol, quickly flipping the pages of her notepad, says, "That's the Take Charge of One Investment rule. In my notes I called it the 'Do it yourself and save rule,' but you can't create your own annuity, can you?"

"No, not entirely, but you can get surprisingly close and save a lot of money along the way. By the end of our discussion, I think that you'll see what I mean. But first let's set the groundwork and get an understanding of the products offered by insurance companies."

Annuities are divided into three basic categories: fixed, variable, and indexed. During the withdrawal period, annuities offer guaranteed income under the provisions outlined within the contract.

If you are considering buying an annuity, remember the discussion of guarantees and their related costs from Chapter 1: *If an annuity or any insurance-based product has a feature or benefit, the feature or benefit comes at a cost.*

Determining that cost is no small task. No one can hold a candle to the insurance industry when it comes to taking a simple concept and piling on so many options and features that comparing one company's product with another can be nearly impossible. To address this problem, we'll limit this discussion to the most basic product features.

Costs and Tax Treatment of Annuity Contracts

One key tax feature of insurance products is that the IRS allows for a tax-deferred buildup of gains inside life insurance products. Even though an annuity is much more a savings or investment product than it is insurance, insurance companies are anxious to retain the tax-deferred treatment of any gains that might be earned while holding the annuity contract. To be sure annuities qualify for the same tax-deferred internal buildup granted to insurance products, the insurance companies presented the concept of annuities to the IRS as a retirement-planning vehicle.

The IRS went along. In doing so, however, the IRS lumped annuity contracts in with other tax-qualified savings plans and restricted withdrawals from an annuity contract before age fifty-nine and a half. Investors can withdraw from an annuity prior to that age, but they are charged income tax on the amount of the earnings that they withdraw (at ordinary rates), plus a 10 percent tax penalty.

You, Your Annuity, and the IRS

The IRS allows annuity contracts additional tax privileges. Even though the IRS considers annuities to be a retirement vehicle, unlike the annual contribution restrictions on IRAs and 401(k) plans, there is no limit on the amount that may be invested in an annuity, and there is no mandatory forced withdrawal schedule as is found in a traditional IRA. In addition, as with any asset class, an annuity contract may be transferred to a spouse at the time of death on a stepped-up basis without going through probate.

The IRS affords annuity contracts yet one more piece of flexibility: IRS Section 1035 allows for the exchange of annuity contracts without a tax impact. If you invested in an annuity offered by company ABC, and two years later find that you prefer the annuity sold by XYZ Company, Section 1035 permits a tax-free exchange to the XYZ annuity. The requirement is simple: For the exchange to be tax free, you must be sure the funds move directly (or as directly as possible) from ABC to XYZ. If you hold the funds for any length of time, you may trigger a taxable event. It should be noted that even though transferring an annuity is a nontaxable event in the eyes of the IRS, it is a surrender and purchase in the eyes of the annuity companies. Thus, there could be surrender charges leveled by ABC and a new withdrawal restriction period at XYZ (as described in detail below).

Withdrawal Costs During the Accumulation Period

Of course, insurance companies want you to leave your money in the annuity as long as possible. So, in addition to any penalties that may be imposed by the IRS on any early withdrawals of funds, almost every annuity company imposes its own restrictions on withdrawals. These fees generally take the form of a surrender charge, leveled if the owner cancels the annuity contract in the early years. Typically, surrender fees are a percentage of the amount in the account. The surrender fee phases out over a period of between three and ten years.

Annuity companies understand that surrender fees may discourage some people from buying their products. Hence, many companies offer a partial withdrawal provision with no fee. The withdrawal provisions typically allow a once-a-year withdrawal of up to 10 percent of the amount invested. The annuity company usually sets a cap on such withdrawals at 50 percent of the amount invested. Should your withdrawal exceed the provision limits, you can expect to pay a fee on the excess amount.

When you withdraw funds from an annuity, the IRS deems that you are withdrawing the "earnings" first. What does that mean? Let's assume that you're over fifty-nine and a half, and you own a fixed annuity contract in which you invested $35,000. Today that contract is worth $55,000. You withdraw $3,500, or 10 percent of your original investment. (Withdrawal limits typically apply to the amount originally invested rather than the total value of the account.) While a withdrawal of this size keeps you within the company's 10 percent partial withdrawal limit and spares you the surrender fee, you'll still have to pay income tax on your withdrawal of any earnings.

The IRS considers that when you make a withdrawal from an annuity contract, you are withdrawing the income portion first. Hence, in this case, the full $3,500 is treated as earnings and, as such, is taxed at the ordinary income rate. In fact, any withdrawal of money down to the amount of your investment is taxable. If you withdraw that same $3,500 before you are fifty-nine and a half, add an additional $350 (10 percent penalty) to your tax bill. (This IRS rule applies to annuity contracts entered into after 1981; those entered into before that date are treated differently.)

Sales Fees

Surprise! Annuities impose no sales fee. The amount that you invest in an annuity will go to work for you without any fees imposed.

Does that sound great? If so, remember the old saying about things that sound too good to be true. The insurance company earns its money from ongoing fees such as one of the following:

- On fixed annuities, the insurance company earns the spread, which is the difference between the amount it earns by investing your money and the amount it credits to your account.

- On variable annuities, the insurance company imposes a fee for the life insurance portion of the contract plus a somewhat pricey account-management fee.

Each of these has the effect of reducing the amount the annuitant earns on his funds held in the annuity. A more accurate way for insurance companies to present the annuity contract fees would be to say that there is no up-front sale commission charged on the investments; however, there are fees and earning reductions that are taken annually as long as you hold the contract.

So, no up-front sales cost? True. No profit for the insurance company? Don't be silly.

Annuity Time Periods

The ownership of an annuity product is broken down into two time periods:

1. The accumulation period, during which you put money into the account and leave it there to grow.

2. The withdrawal period, during which you take the money out.

Each period has a separate set of rules and its own contract form. You can enter into an accumulation contract without entering into a withdrawal contract, or you can enter into a withdrawal contract only.

For example, you may choose to *accumulate* money inside an annuity contract and at a future date simply withdraw the funds in a lump sum. Or you may transfer your funds from the accumulation contract to a withdrawal contract and begin receiving payments. (The lump-sum withdrawal is most common.)

Most *withdrawal* contracts are funded with a lump-sum contribution.

"I thought options had a lot of moving parts, but they pale in comparison to annuities. There is no way you can do this yourself," says Carol.

"You might feel that annuities are as opaque as mud and as involved as a Rubik's Cube," I tell her. "But fear not—we can explain the basic annuity types quite easily, and I think that as we go forward you will see some opportunities start to emerge."

A Quick Guide to Annuity Types

As mentioned earlier, there are three basic types of annuities:

- Fixed annuities
- Variable annuities
- Equity indexed annuities

Fixed Annuities

During the accumulation period, money invested in a *fixed annuity* earns a fixed rate of return. The (minimum) rate of return is set at the inception of the contract. If you are considering a fixed annuity, you can shop around because different contracts offer different rates. This is no different than when you shop different banks to find a better return on a CD. What affects the rate of return offered by the annuity company?

- The profit margin that the annuity company is seeking

- The competitive nature of the industry

- The length of time you are willing to tie up your funds

- The company's selling costs

What to Consider: A Buyer's Checklist

A straight-up comparison of annuity contracts is difficult because there are so many provisions to the contract and the annuity contract provisions are not uniform from company to company or even from product to product offered by the same company. One place this becomes apparent is the interest rate set on a fixed annuity. Originally, fixed annuities set a "stated rate," which never changed. Now, however, many annuity contracts offer contracts with a rate that follows the market.

This feature may be advantageous or disadvantageous, depending on the direction of the interest rates. For example, some annuity contracts offer a guaranteed rate for a relatively short period—say one year—then a floating rate thereafter (great for the contract holder if interest rates move up). Other contracts lock in an interest rate for six, seven, or ten years or for the lifetime of the holder (good for investors if interest rates fall). Some contracts even roll the interest rate using a method traditionally called *laddering*, in which a certain portion of the investment comes due each year and is reinvested at the then-current interest rate. Every fixed annuity contract offers a set minimum return; in effect, this is a rate that will be maintained by the insurance company no matter how low the general interest rate falls.

How do you decide which to buy? Your decision should be based on your opinion about the state of the economy. Do you believe that interest rates will go up? If so, then buy an annuity with a short-term locked-in interest rate. If you think interest rates will decline, you should select the longer-term guarantees.

Beyond these general guidelines, here's a checklist of what to consider when buying a fixed annuity:

- The guaranteed minimum interest rate that the annuity contract is offering

- How (and if) returns will be adjusted during the contract

- Withdrawal restrictions, generally set as a number of years

- Partial withdrawal allowances restrictions

Take special note of these last two items. Withdrawal restrictions vary from company to company and contract to contract. *Read the withdrawal restrictions section of your contract carefully!* You don't want to buy a contract with an eight-year withdrawal restriction if you think that you may want or need to withdraw a large portion of your money in three years.

The Medicaid Qualified Annuity

An important subset of the fixed annuity is the Medicaid qualified annuity. There is no requirement that a Medicaid qualified annuity be a fixed annuity. However, I have never seen any other form of annuity used for this purpose.

To qualify for Medicaid benefits, a person's assets must be substantially depleted. The government sets strict limits on the amount of assets and income a person may hold and still qualify to receive benefits. Many people align their finances in such a way to qualify for Medicaid benefits. Making early gifts of assets is highly effective and incurs almost no cost if done within the IRS guidelines.

Another tool that can be used to deplete a person's includable assets is the Medicaid qualified annuity. By purchasing a Medicaid qualified annuity, the buyer is in effect removing funds from his or her own control, thus reducing the amount of their countable assets. An annuity must meet the following requirements to be Medicaid qualified:

1. The annuity must be nonassignable and nontransferable.

2. The annuity must be an immediate payout type.

3. The annuity must predate the start of Medicaid benefits.

4. The amount received (generally the monthly payments) when combined with the person's other income (generally Social Security) must not exceed the maximum monthly income allowable under Medicaid.

If you are interested in learning more about these annuities, a good book on the topic is *Medicaid Planning Handbook,* by Alexander Bove.

Not every annuity company offers Medicaid qualified annuities. Some companies that do are listed here:

- American General

- Fidelity & Guaranty

- GE Capital

- Jefferson Pilot

- Standard Life of Indiana

Variable Annuities

Fundamentally, a variable annuity is a mutual fund wrapped inside an insurance policy. When buying a variable annuity, you will be asked to select the type of subaccount, or separate account, in which you want your funds invested. You can think of the subaccounts as you would think about different types of mutual funds—balanced portfolios, bond portfolios, aggressive growth portfolios, and so on. As with all annuity products, variable annuities receive deferred-income tax treatment. In effect, capital gains and dividend income build up inside the annuity on a tax-deferred basis during the accumulation period.

You can fund a variable annuity with a single large payment or with individual payments over a period of time. A portion of your money goes to the subaccount (mutual fund) you've chosen, and a portion provides insurance guaranteeing that if you die before withdrawing assets from the annuity, your beneficiary will be paid either the current value of the separate account or the amount you invested, whichever is greater. The cost of the insurance is typically about 1 percent of the amount invested.

Adding up the Costs and Making Your Choice

In addition to the insurance cost, companies charge a "separate account" management fee for variable annuity contracts. Management fees are coming down (due to the unwanted attention they have been attracting), but they are still high. Assume that the management fee for a variable annuity will be about double the management costs of a typical mutual fund.

The next cost is the surrender or withdrawal fees that the insurance company charges to discourage you from withdrawing funds or closing out your contract for a period of time—typically the first four to eight years of the accumulation period.

These fees aside, the one thing that disturbs me most regarding this product is that it is next to impossible to come across an owner of a variable annuity who can explain to you exactly what it is that she has bought. The product's design is too confusing. The Met Life Variable Annuity prospectus is over 500 pages long; that's 280 pages longer than the classic novel *To Kill a Mockingbird*, and Met Life's opus is not nearly as well written as Harper Lee's.

Selecting a variable annuity contract is more difficult than selecting a fixed annuity from among its peers. That's because the critical factor in choosing a variable annuity is the investment results of the separate account, and a company that had above-average performance in its separate accounts last year may not repeat itself next year.

Equity Indexed Annuities

In a nutshell, this type of investment really does offer "peace of mind at a price." Equity indexed annuities (EIAs, sometimes also called financial indexed annuities or FIAs) offer some very interesting features that deserve consideration by investors. However, these features come at a significant cost that you should fully investigate before you buy.

Unfortunately, the fee structure is complicated. Insurance companies are not the Ritz Hotel. If you have ever stayed at a Ritz, you likely enjoyed the hotel's superior level of service, the plush lobby, the efficient staff, the excellent restaurants, and luxurious rooms. Sure, it all comes at a price, but don't worry—the price is clearly stated in advance so that you can make up your mind how you want to spend or save your money. There's no guesswork when you get your bill. The Ritz is happy and willing to detail the cost of its service on a clear statement upon checkout or even during your stay.

Sadly, insurance companies do not operate that way. Computing the cost of owning an EIA is a challenge worthy of a graduate-level actuary.

During the accumulation period, an EIA allows you to invest in the equity market and *never suffer from a down market*. (Now, that's not a bad idea.) To get that benefit, however, you must be willing to give up part of any gains you may earn during a good (up) market.

EIA contracts are written to offer the investor a guaranteed minimum return—generally between 0 to 4 percent (4 percent is high and fairly rare in today's market). This product, therefore, has the safety element.

In addition, EIAs offers the potential for an equity kick, based on the performance of the market. If the index to which the annuity is compared (such as the S&P 500) increases in value, a portion of the increase will be credited to the investor's account. Here's an example.

You deposit $100,000. The EIA contract you have selected calls for a minimum return of 0 (even if the market declines) and a maximum return of 60 percent of any increase in the S&P 500. The following table is an oversimplification of this scenario and is for clarification purposes only.

	Market Result	Account Balance
Day-one deposit $100,000	—	$100,000
End of year one	S&P down 1%	$100,000
End of year two	S&P up 11%	$106,660
End of year three	S&P down 8%	$106,660
End of year four	S&P up 15%	$116,259

Note: Remember that only 60 percent of the S&P 500's gains are credited. Also, in real life, you would have less than $116,259 because this chart does not account for the annual management fee (about $2,000 to $2,500) or the annual insurance costs (about $800 to $1,000 a year).

From this chart, it is clear that in year one, the market went down, but your account did not suffer; it was still worth $100,000. When the market went up, however, your account increased by a portion of the increase in market value of the index to which your contract is pegged (here, the S&P 500).

How much of the market increase will end up in your account? That varies from company to company. At some companies, the increase credited to your account is a percentage of the total increase of the index, such as 60 percent, 65 percent, or 70 percent. Other companies cap the increase at a percentage, such as 12 percent a year.

Comparing Annuities and Considering a Do-It-Yourself Alternative

Fixed annuities are the safest type of annuity. They allow an investor to predict with a good deal of certainty when and how much will be available to him or her. There is no risk of a down market eroding your assets. However, with a do-it-yourself approach, you can avoid the costs of ownership during the accumulation period. You may want to consider buying term insurance and investing in high-grade corporate or government bonds that may offer a higher return than the annuity contract. The cost of a term life insurance policy is incredibly inexpensive and the returns from the high-grade bonds you buy are very reliable.

Among annuity contracts, Variable annuities are the best selection for a long-term investor. The track record for the stock market over long periods such as twenty, thirty, or forty years has been impressive. However, variable annuity buyers may also want to consider a do-it-yourself approach of buying term insurance and investing regularly in a good mutual fund. This will provide two benefits. First, the lower total management costs will leave more of the earnings for you, and secondly there is no "lock-up" period when withdrawing funds would incur a penalty.

Equity indexed annuities offer an interesting middle ground in performance between fixed and variable annuities. Historically, over the long run, a variable annuity will outperform an indexed annuity. The problem is that the variable annuity subaccount value fluctuates with the market. Hence, at the very time the investor wants to withdraw or annuitize her funds, the value of the account may be depressed. The do-it-yourself approach for an equity indexed annuity is slightly more complex, requiring three steps:

- Buy a term life insurance policy
- Buy high-grade bonds.
- Buy long-term S&P calls.

Is the "Do-it-Yourself" Approach Right for You?

Annuities offer a neat package to achieve a goal. Yet they have two problems:

- High costs can result in reduced performance to the investor.
- Most have long lock-up periods.

The do-it-yourself route will outperform the insurance company packaged product, but is that approach right for you? Only you can answer that question. You know, for example, that it is less expensive to paint your house yourself than to hire a painter to do the work. Nevertheless, if you hate painting, or you do not like to climb on ladders, you might hire a painter. Having someone else do the work of investing our money for us costs more, but for some people, it may be worth the extra expense.

Either choice—doing it yourself or paying the fee—has merit. The important point is that you have two options. The wise investor will consider both before making a decision.

Anne interrupts me with a very good question. "It seems that the real advantage to accumulating money inside an annuity is that there is a deferral of the income tax on the earnings. However, I have been accumulating money in my 401(k), which is also tax deferred and probably has a lower management cost. Am I missing something here? Should I switch from putting money in my 401(k) and instead accumulate my money in an annuity?"

"No, Anne you are not missing a thing," I respond. "Building up your funds inside your 401(k) is more efficient than investing the same dollars in an annuity contract. And don't forget that your employer is probably also contributing to your 401(k)."

"So, if I am considering an annuity contract, it's OK to build up my funds outside the annuity and when I am ready to begin withdrawing funds buy an annuity contract that will guarantee to pay me for life," says Anne with a question in her voice.

"Yes," I respond. "That's called an immediate annuity because you buy it one month and the next month it starts to pay."

"Anne, now that you have brought it up let's talk about the withdrawal phase of an annuity next," I add.

Withdrawing Money from Your Annuity

Now let's take some money out of this contract. Remember you may fund a distribution annuity contract either by accumulating funds in an annuity contract (described in the previous section) or by a lump-sum investment. Once you accept the first payment from the annuity company, the contract is said to be annuitized. Once annuitized, the contract is pretty much written in stone; the flexibility afforded to you during the accumulation period is gone. Therefore, before you take that first check, you need to make three big decisions:

1. How do you want your payments—monthly, quarterly, or annually?

2. How do you want the funds held during the withdrawal phase? If they are held in a fixed account, you can be sure of the payout. If they are in a variable account, the payments will fluctuate. You hope that they fluctuate upward at a pace equal to or faster than the rate of inflation, but there is no guarantee.

3. How long do you want the checks to keep coming? For five years, ten years, twenty years, or for the rest of your life? (Payout options are reviewed on page 143.)

Your individual needs and circumstances will help direct the decisions you make. One factor that all of us must consider, however, is how much of a bite Uncle Same will take from our annuity payouts.

Taxation During the Annuity Payout Period

Unlike the partial withdrawal during the accumulation period described earlier in this chapter (in which the first dollar taken is considered to be earnings and is fully taxable at your ordinary income tax rate), when you annuitize the annuity contract, the IRS allows you to apportion the income. Using what it calls the *exclusion ratio*, the IRS takes the amount of time you have elected to receive funds—five years, ten years, your lifetime, or any other specified period of time—and uses that period to compute the amount of each annuity payment you receive that is a return of your own capital. That amount is excluded from taxation. (In the case of a lifetime payout option, the IRS simply uses a mortality table to determine your exclusion ratio.) The exclusion ratio allows you to spread out your taxes over a longer period of time.

Let's say that you select a lifetime payout. Using the IRS mortality table, you determine that, based on your life expectancy, your monthly checks will be made up of 41.5 percent return of capital and 58.5 percent income. (The insurance company or your CPA will do this computation for you.) Your exclusion ratio, therefore, is 41.5 percent of the amount received from the annuity company. You will be taxed (at the ordinary income tax rate) only on the remainder of what you receive, 58.5 percent.

The above computation is for a fixed annuity. The computation to withdraw funds from a variable contract is more complex and requires a recalculation each month depending on the amount you receive. Each year, the insurance company will send you an IRS Form 1099 so you know how much is taxable.

What about that 10 percent IRS penalty for withdrawing your funds prior to age fifty-nine and a half? At any age, if you decide to annuitize the contract (that is, you agree to accept regular payments), the IRS will base the income tax impact on the exclusion ratio method; no 10 percent penalty will apply. There are two other ways the penalty can be avoided: if the annuitant becomes totally disabled, or if he or she dies. (And you thought the IRS didn't have a heart.)

Annuity Withdrawal Options

When it comes to payouts, annuity companies are externally flexible. No matter what combination of payout needs you may have, the annuity company will be able to structure a payment plan that will suit your goals. The most common options include the following:

- Fixed number of years: This option works best for individuals or couples who are seeking funds for a set period of time, say until a pension payout begins or until a large debt can be collected. The investor can select any period of time—one year, forty-three years, you name it. The annuity company will be happy to oblige by creating a contract that aligns with the requested time frame.

- Lifetime: Select this option if you want to receive checks for the rest of your life. The checks will stop coming at your death. That's simple enough. You are not required to name yourself as the annuitant; you could name your spouse, your child, a friend, or the guy who lives next door. The only obligation is that the person you name is a real living person, not a corporation or an entity with a perpetual life. Remember, however, that when you select a lifetime payout option, any funds not distributed because of your early demise belong to the annuity company. (Ouch!)

- Joint or last survivor: Couples frequently select this type of contract because it will pay as long as either person is alive. The second person may be a spouse, child, relative, friend, or anyone else you may choose. In most cases, the amount paid out does not change after the first death.

- Lifetime with a period certain: Some people don't like the uncertainty of a lifetime payout. If they die soon after taking out the contract, the annuity company gets to keep the balance (the unremitted portion) of the funds. Anyone who is uncomfortable with this concept could consider a lifetime payout with period certain. Here, payments are made until the annuitant dies or for a certain period, whichever is longer. A lifetime payout with ten years certain, for example, guarantees that, if the annuitant dies in the twenty-second month, his beneficiary will receive ninety-eight more monthly payments (for a total of 120 months or ten years). If the annuitant dies in the 115th month, the beneficiary will receive five monthly payments. If the annuitant lives past the 120th monthly payment, the contract will function just like a lifetime payout option and thus stop making payments at the time of the annuitant's death.

You can choose from an almost endless variety of payout options.

Weighing the Costs and Potential Benefits

What can you expect your annuity to cost, and what kind of return can you expect from your investment? We have covered most of the fees incurred in the ownership of an annuity, but let's take a moment now to review them:

- Mortality fee: This pays for the insurance that guarantees that at the annuitant's death (during the accumulation period) the account value will be no less than the amount invested. The fee ranges from 25 to 100 basis points of the value of your account each year (100 basis points = 1 percent). The catch is that even if the annuity account has grown to be a greater value than the amount invested, the insurance company goes on collecting this fee. In addition, because the insurance premium amount collected can be a percentage of the total in the account, the premiums can increase each year, even as there is a reduced need for the insurance.

- Account maintenance fees: Generally $0 to $50 a quarter.

- Penalties for early withdrawal: These vary; however, this penalty will generally phase out after about four or five years in a fixed annuity and six to eight years for a variable.

- Account management fees: Most noticeable in the variable annuity and equity indexed products, these fees average about 1.5 percent to 2.75 percent per year.

- Return caps: Found in equity indexed annuities, these caps limit the investor's return. Any return exceeding cap belongs to the annuity company.

I tread lightly in describing what you can expect from an annuity contract because there are so many elements that will impact the result. However, here is a very broad example.

For a sixty-five-year-old male who deposits a $100,000 lump sum in a fixed annuity and selects the immediate monthly lifetime payment option, a reasonable payout expectation is about $850 per month. Because females are assumed to live longer than males, a female selecting the same contract could expect to receive about $790 to $800 a month.

As with any investment tool, your circumstances and your other investments will determine whether or not an annuity is right for you.

I see that both Anne and Mark are making some notes and others have begun to shift in their seats. I suggest that we all get up and pour that last cup of coffee before we move on.

"What's next?" asks Tim.

"We should talk a bit about market fraud," I say.

"Are you really sure that is a good use of our time? I only want to know how to make money. I can't believe that spending our time to talk about market fraud will be meaningful to any of us," says Tim.

13: If You Become a Victim of Fraud

How to Keep Your Money from Vanishing

It would be nice if there was no need to discuss this topic, but it is necessary. Well-meaning investors sometime lose money for reasons other than market risk. Imagine how you would feel if someone else's fraudulent act wiped out your savings. Before I launch into this topic, I want to be clear. The vast majority of investment salespeople are ethical and hard working. The number of complaints filed against brokers and insurance agents each year as compared to the number of transactions is minimal.

Frauds against investors can be broken down into three categories:

- Too good to be true: "I've got a 20 percent bank-guaranteed CD I can offer you."

- Corporate frauds: Such as what happened at Enron and WorldCom.

- Brokerage account fraud: A broker may churn your account or make unauthorized trades.

Too Good to Be True

I place this type of fraud first because it is easy to fall for one of these schemes. Call it greed or hubris, it happens every day and often to people who believe that they know better. Your State Security Department can probably give you a list of the current scams. Recently, one of the more popular is this. Someone contacts an investor and says, "There is a bank CD that is paying double or triple the interest rate you're earning right now. Because the CD is being sold by a bank, you know that your money is guaranteed."

"How could this be?" the trusting victim asks.

"Because the bank is located in the Caribbean and is not restricted by those pesky U.S. government regulations," the con artist replies.

The unsuspecting investor is anxious to improve his returns and so hands over a check for $10,000, $50,000, or more. He'll likely receive interest for the first few months. Then the checks stop coming, and the money is gone. This type of scheme is so common in all its variations that it even has a name—it's called a Ponzi scheme.

There Really Was a Ponzi

Carlo (Charles) Ponzi, a native of Italy, arrived in America at the age of fifteen. Ponzi was bright and personable, although not always morally well tuned. (In 1908, he received a twenty-month sentence in Toronto for forgery. Ponzi was released from jail early. In 1910, he received a twenty-four-month sentence in Atlanta for smuggling five illegal aliens into America via Canada.) The industrious Ponzi worked many jobs, including dishwasher, store clerk, and interpreter. By 1917, at the age of thirty-five, he had settled in Boston, where he worked as a letter writer for illiterate immigrants. During this time, Ponzi decided to start a newsletter about exporting goods to America. He sent letters to foreign businesses to see if they were interested in subscribing. One businessman from Spain sent back a letter asking that Ponzi forward him a sample copy. The businessman included a postal coupon he had purchased in Spain. The coupon could be exchanged for U.S. postage at the post office. Lightning struck when Ponzi realized that due to the weak currency in Spain, the postal coupon had been bought for the equivalent of one U.S. cent. When he exchanged it for U.S. postage, he received stamps worth six cents. Eureka! Ponzi reasoned that if he had $100, he could convert it to foreign currency, buy foreign postal coupons, convert them to U.S. postage, and sell the stamps at face value—thus netting about 400 percent after all costs. But there was a little obstacle; Ponzi did not have $100.

No problem. Ponzi told all his friends, neighbors, and everyone else who would listen about his "system for earning big profits." He soon printed brochures and opened an office on Court Street in downtown Boston. The business plan he described was simple. He would do all the work of buying the foreign postal coupons, converting them to U.S. postage, and reselling the stamps. He would use the investors' money and return to them a 50 percent return in ninety days. (He later changed it to a 50 percent return in forty-five days.)

People liked the idea. They liked it so much that they asked if they could be investors. Early investors were paid the 50 percent return, just as promised. Word spread, and it was off to the races. The money poured in. Soon Ponzi was greeted by a line of investors at his office door each morning, each hoping that he would accept their money. Ponzi was willing to accept investments as small as $10. The average investment was slightly less than $300, a large sum for the day. One man took the train to Boston from St. Louis to give his money to Ponzi; investors included judges, government officials, and clergy. People applauded when Ponzi walked by on the streets of Boston. Women asked for a piece of his clothing and sent marriage proposals. Business leaders sought his advice.

At the peak of Ponzi's scheme, money came in at the rate of almost $100,000 a week. (Remember that this was in 1919.) A staff of clerks was hired to keep track of money, but they soon gave up and simply piled the cash in boxes to be sorted out later. When it ended on July 26, 1920, Ponzi had taken in slightly over $15 million (approximately $201 million in 2007 dollars). He had received enough money from investors to buy 18 billion postal coupons. Records show that he bought just two. The total value of the coupons he bought was twelve cents.

Ponzi served three and a half years of a five-year jail sentence. When he was released, he packed up and moved to Florida. There he set up a land business. Changing his name to Charles Borelli, he bought land for $16 an acre, subdivided it into twenty-three lots per acre, and sold the lots to out-of-state investors for $10 each. Each sale came with a promise that each lot would be worth $5,300 in two years. Ponzi sold almost 500 lots. The real estate lots that he sold are still right where they were at the time of the sales: under several feet of swamp water.

Ponzi died in Rio de Janeiro in 1949 leaving an estate of $75, which he had saved to pay for his funeral expenses.

The story of Ponzi is more than simple fluff. It is a cautionary tale we should consider each time we hear something that's too good. The Ponzi story is repeated every day. There are elements of the Ponzi scheme in the Jim and Tammy Faye Bakker fraud. They sold 100 times the Lifetime Lodging Memberships they could have delivered even in the most ideal situation. By using television, the Bakkers were able to raise $168,000,000 from 150,000 well-meaning individuals. It is interesting that when taking into account the inflation of the dollar, the amount raised by the Bakkers was similar to that accumulated by Ponzi.

The Ponzi scheme, along with its many variations, is by far the most common type of greed-driven fraud. Another type of too-good-to-be-true fraud is the "selling what isn't really there" scam. Generally, this scam involves a bogus oil well or gold mine. However, the product could be anything of value. Here is an example.

In the 1970s, the price of precious stones, especially diamonds, spiked in value. People who knew nothing about gems were suddenly interested in diamonds as an investment. Some people actually mortgaged their homes to invest in stones. This feeding frenzy brought out some con artists in Phoenix, Arizona. They offered to sell high-quality diamonds with a money-back guarantee. If the value of the stones ever dropped, the company would buy them back for the full price the investor had paid. There was one catch. The investors were told that the stones were of such high quality that they came in a sealed opaque pouch. If the seal was broken or damaged, the guarantee would be void. That's right; you guessed it. There were no diamonds. Each pouch held nothing more than a piece of cut glass. By the time the fraud was discovered, the perpetrators were long gone. They got away with at least $15 million. It may have been much more, as state regulators believe that many who were swindled were too embarrassed to come forward.

What the Government Has Done

Generally, this class of fraud is dealt with at the state level. (Jim and Tammy Faye Bakker were an exception, as they were prosecuted in federal court.) States make a feeble attempt to warn people of common frauds, but as a practical matter they are unaware that a fraud is taking place until a victim complains. By that time it is usually too late. The saddest feature of many frauds is that they target seniors.

What You Can Do

Let your common sense, not your desire for a large return, be your guiding force. I am not saying that every promised large return is a fraud. But when we hear of an oversized return or an investment that comes with many guarantees, it's time to carefully examine the offering. If you are investing a lot of money, consider taking the offering document to your attorney for review.

Also, remember the Nine Rules of Successful Investing, especially Rule One, "Invest in What You Know," and Rule Three, "Embrace the Learning Curve."

Fraud at the Corporate Level

Some of the corporate frauds that we have seen in the past decade are downright shocking. In the past ten years, millions of investors have lost billions of dollars because they invested their money in companies that provided fraudulent information.

On October 15, 2001, Enron had the seventh largest market value of any company in America, larger than IBM, GM, or Coke. On October 16, 2001, Enron made a public announcement that it was reviewing its books for possible accounting irregularities. Just six weeks later, on December 2, 2001, the company declared bankruptcy, shutting its doors and thus wiping out the investment of tens of thousands of people. In less than thirty business days, the loss to Enron investors had added up to over $60 billion.

On June 25, 2002, WorldCom restated its earnings. The restatement eventually turned out to be a reduction of $11 billion. The restatements, which came in waves, devastated the price of the stock. Again, tens of thousands of investors lost billions of dollars.

These are not isolated cases: In each case, investors were the victims.

Why Do These Problems Happen?

It's the system. Look at how a public corporation is structured:

- The shareholders are the owners; they want their stock to go up in value.

- The shareholders elect the board of directors, which is bound to work in the shareholder's interest.

- The board hires the company president, often offering rich rewards based on company earnings or stock price appreciation.

In 2005, Rupert Murdoch, head of NewsCorp, earned a $25 million bonus based on the company's improved earnings per share, but that's peanuts. In 2004, Terry Semel, CEO of Yahoo, was paid $230 million; in 2001 Larry Ellison, CEO of Oracle, made $706 million. In the five years from 1999 to 2004, Sandy Weill of Citigroup earned over $754 million in bonuses. In 1998, Michael Eisner, then head of Disney, earned a bonus of $570 million on top of his salary. Eisner's bonus was based on an increase in the value of the company stock. In 2005, Dr. William McGuire of UnitedHealth enjoyed a salary of $8 million, but that was barely pocket change. McGuire's unrealized capital gains on his company stock options were $1.6 billion—yes, that's *billion.*

I am not saying that Murdoch, Semel, Ellison, Weil, Eisner, or McGuire did anything illegal. However, with prizes like these, isn't it possible that some people might look the other way if the accounting department found an opportunity to inflate the earnings number? Or, possibly, might even encourage the accounting department to be a bit creative? It's not just the money, either. For leadership, corporations tend to look for hard-charging opportunity seekers who like being in first place. Being president of a fast-growing company brings respect, praise, rock-star-level adulation, and your picture on the cover of *BusinessWeek*. CNBC talks about you in the morning, and *Barron's* writes about you on the weekend. If your company is showing large enough profits, no one seems to ask why you took the company jet to Toronto for the day to watch your favorite team play the Expos.

The body charged with the responsibility of overseeing the ethical operation of a public company is the board of directors. Yet being a board member is not a full-time job, and it frequently pays relatively little.

What the Government Has Done

At best, government regulations are reactive rather than proactive. From the Securities Exchange Act of 1933 through the Sarbanes-Oxley of 2002, legislative safeguards have historically been based on frauds that have already taken place. The Sarbanes-Oxley Act is sweeping and impressive. However, next week, next month, or next year some company president or chief financial officer will come up with a new way around the system.

What You Can Do to Protect Your Money

The answer is surprisingly simple. Remember and apply the Nine Rules of Successful Investing. For example, Rule Five, "Create a Complementary Combination of Investments," helps you build a diversified portfolio. The people who were crushed by the Enron fraud, for instance, held too much of a single investment. Following Rule Nine, "Rebalance Your Portfolio," would have helped millions of people protect billions of dollars. Each of the companies listed above had tremendous increases in their stock value prior to their collapse. By following Rule Nine and frequently rebalancing their portfolios, investors would have sold off much of the inflated stock before its value vanished.

At the Broker-Dealer Level

Compare the number of client complaints filed annually against broker-dealers to the trillions of dollars that are traded, and it becomes clear that the brokerage industry has a very low complaint rate.

Client complaints against a broker-dealer fall into five categories:

- Violations of the Suitability Rule

- Fraud

- Churning

- Unauthorized trades

- Selling away

- Failure to supervise

Suitability Rule

A broker is prohibited from making a recommendation to a client to invest in or purchase a security if that recommendation is unsuitable. The concept of suitability takes into consideration the client's age, investment objectives, financial situation, and level of investing experience. How is the broker-dealer supposed to know all this about the client? It's his or her job.

Typically, the broker-dealer starts with the new account form, which includes a list of questions. The client's answers provide the broker-dealer with information about the client. An important question on the new account form is, "What is your investment objective?" Far too many clients check the aggressive-growth option with little real thought. This is unfortunate. Should the account lose money, the broker-dealer can use the client's own statement on the new account form to excuse making speculative recommendations.

You may contact your broker at any time and ask to update or change the information on your account form.

The Suitability Rule extends to making a recommendation of an investment when the investment itself (not the client) is unsuitable. Let's consider an example. A broker-dealer is holding a large inventory of a certain company's stock. The broker-dealer learns that the company is about to be investigated for accounting irregularities. Instead of holding the stock in its inventory, the broker-dealer recommends the stock to its clients. In this case it is the investment that is offered that is unsuitable.

Many years ago, the definition of a recommendation was limited to direct statements, such as this: "Mr. Smith, I think you should buy 500 shares of GM right now." However, the definition has now widened to include content of broker-dealer mailings, Web site content, and comments made at seminars. Some states have gone so far (I think wrongly) as to say that the statement, "You should diversify your portfolio" is a recommendation, and thus the person making the statement may be liable for any investor loss.

The Suitability Rule has even extended to situations where no recommendation is made. Let's say Joe waltzes into a broker's office with $25,000 in cash. The asset represents a lawsuit settlement and is all the money Joe has. Last night on television, Joe saw some guy jumping up and down screaming, "Buy stock in this new company, Squid-in-a-Can!"

Now here comes Joe, who wants to invest all the money he possesses in one stock because he heard about it on television. The courts have ruled that the broker may have liability if he accepts an order when he has reason to believe that the trade is unsuitable based on the client's financial situation.

Fraud

Most of the fraud matters that come before the Financial Industry Regulatory Authority (FINRA) Dispute Resolution Panel are based on "omission of a material fact." In other words, the broker failed to disclose a material piece of information about the investment to the client. (FINRA is the new name of the organization formerly known as the NASD. In the following discussion of current policy matters, the new name will be used.)

Churning

Churning is excessive trading in a client's account. What is wrong with churning? It runs up the broker's fees, thus reducing or even eliminating your return. Now and then, the press will report on a churning case. Generally, the story will be about some poor soul who gave his broker "account discretion." Account discretion is written permission given by a client to a broker allowing the broker to make investment decisions on the client's behalf. Such accounts are common and usually do not cause problems. However, as a practical matter the majority of churning complaints are filed on nondiscretionary accounts.

The best antidote against churning is for investors to carefully read their monthly account statements and be sure they understand every fee and immediately question those that seem unreasonable. It is better to take action as soon as a broker begins churning your account than to discover it six months later.

The brightest red flag to watch for is the purchase, sale, and repurchase of the same or similar security over a short period. If you suspect churning, take two steps. Find a new broker *fast,* and file a complaint with the broker-dealer seeking the return of all fees charged to your account, plus the amount of capital gains you would have made if the investment had remained in place and not been churned. You may not get full satisfaction, but you'll likely get something.

Unauthorized Trades

An unauthorized trade is a trade made in your account without your prior approval. Such trades are completely legal *if* you opened a discretionary account, giving your broker/dealer authority to make trades for you. If you did not, all trades must receive your prior approval. The most common defense offered by brokers in these cases goes something like, "The customer told me that he doesn't understand the market and that I should do whatever I think is best."

The legal remedy for unauthorized trades is straightforward. The brokerage firm must rescind all trades and put the account back in the position that it would have been in, in the absences of the unauthorized trades.

During a FINRA arbitration of an unauthorized trades matter, you may find that it comes down to your word against the broker's. Much of your communications with a broker will take place on the phone, and not all calls are recorded. It is up to you to take good notes of your conversations. In the absences of a tape recording, frequently it is the side that has kept the best notes that wins in arbitration.

Selling Away

Selling away sends a chill down the spine of every brokerage compliance officer. It is a serious problem, and it seems to be getting worse. Selling away is when an agent (a broker or a registered representative) knowingly offers or sells an investment product that is not generally offered by his broker-dealer. The practice is permitted only in cases where the broker-dealer has given the representative written permission, and such permission is rare.

Why do you as an investor care if the salesperson was selling away? Because if the investment being sold is not a product offered by the broker-dealer, you have nowhere to turn should things go awry.

Why would a broker sell away? Typically, it is because these products pay a generous commission. It is surprising how often selling-away investments turn out badly for the investor.

The best defense is to always be alert to anything that seems too good to be true, smells fishy, or suddenly is available only to you.

Red Flags You Should Watch For

A change in the payment process. Let's say that when you invest, you always make your check payable to the name of the broker-dealer. This time, however, the salesperson asks you to make out your check directly to the company. Worse yet, he says, "Just make the check out directly to me, and I'll take care of everything."

If you generally buy through a broker-dealer, there is a paper trail you have become accustomed to. Maybe this time the sales literature looks different, or the confirmation of trade looks different or—where was your head?—you didn't even get a confirmation.

Another common clue is that the broker seems to "know these guys well." That may be just fine. However, this comment seems to come up too often when victims recall a bad selling-away trade.

Failure to Supervise

Let's say that you have had the unfortunate experience of finding out the hard way that your broker was less than honest. Maybe he or she churned your account, made unsuitable recommendations, or made unauthorized trades in your account.

Under the broad category of rules titled "Supervision," the broker-dealership is responsible for the actions, communications, and sales tactics of its registered representatives.

Your lawyer loves this rule because it allows her to drag the broker-dealership into any case you have against the broker. That's good for you, as the broker-dealership is usually the deep pockets in the dispute.

What to Do When Things Go Wrong

If you discover an offense and the violation is clear—for example, the broker made an unauthorized trade in your account—contact the broker and convey the following:

- The broker must stop all trading in this account now.

- You expect 100 percent restoration made to the account within forty-eight hours. Immediately after your phone conversation with the broker, follow up with a written letter to the broker and the branch manager.

If you don't, the broker may claim you never called him or that you did call but never asked him to correct the account. Put your demands in writing.

- When the restoration is made, close the account.

- If the restoration is not made, close the account.

Whatever happens, close the account. In arbitration, victims commonly say, "I found a bunch of errors, but the broker asked me to keep my account active. Then these other things happened, and now most of my money is gone."

Close the account now. It will not weaken your case against the broker, and it may save you from further losses because of the broker's continued unethical activity.

What should you do if you're just suspicious that the broker is not acting in your best interest? Close the account. Perhaps later you will determine exactly what was bothering you. For now, it is simply best to get out of the situation that is making you uncomfortable. Remember: *It's your money.*

Writing the Complaint Letter

People are of two minds on this matter. Should you write the first letter, or should you hire an attorney? The quick letter that you dash off to the branch manager will generally be answered with a standard denial letter. Don't worry—it's just a form letter, and you can continue to pursue the matter. However, if the amount of money involved is large, it is worth the time and cost to hire an attorney with experience in pursuing matters of broker fraud. Either way, always submit your complaint in writing.

If you write the complaint letter yourself, here are a few things to keep in mind:

- It does not need to be a long letter.

- Include dates and the names of the people involved.

- State your complaint, but leave it open ended. For example, tell why it is that you are complaining and add that your grievance is not limited to this event. (Once you find one thing wrong in your account, more ugly surprises may pop up as you look deeper. You don't want to limit your ability to collect for other transgressions that you may find with additional research.)

- When asking for an amount of money, explain how you computed the amount and add that this is a minimum based on this event and in no way limits your ability to seek additional funds if further research reveals additional transgressions.

- Set a deadline. I like forty-eight hours (unless you want more time to complete your research).

- Request a written response to your letter.

Send the letter to the branch manager. (You may copy the broker; that is up to you.) You may or may not feel that you need to send a copy of the letter to the brokerage home office until you get a response from the local branch manager. Sometimes it's best to handle these situations locally. There is no need to send a copy of your letter to FINRA or the SEC at this time. A letter to the authorities at this early stage may just slow things down. Remember that you have given the local broker and branch manager a very short time to fix the problem. In just a few days, you will know if you will need to contact the broker-dealer's home office and finally FINRA.

If you hire an attorney to represent you, find one with experience in this field. The hourly rate for an experienced securities arbitration attorney varies from city to city. The contingency rate (if you go that route) may surprise you. Don't expect the customary 30 percent or 33 percent you hear in personal injury cases. The contingency rate may run 40 percent, 45 percent, or as high as 50 percent. The logic is that typically the amounts collected in securities fraud matters are smaller than the amounts awarded in a personal injury case; hence, contingency rates need to be larger.

Going to Arbitration

If your letters to the broker-dealership do not bring you satisfaction you may need to submit your claim to the FINRA Dispute Resolution Panel.

There are advantages to settling disputes through the FINRA panel. The system is very low in cost, straightforward, and relatively fast. Going to court is expensive, complex, and can be very time consuming. Another advantage is that the arbitrators are knowledgeable in securities regulation and in the practical application of sales tactics.

If you decide to seek arbitration because your broker has knowingly taken an action (or led you to take action) that was unethical, your first step is to visit the FINRA Web site at *www.finra.org*. Click on the tab titled "Arbitration & Mediation." The page that opens will guide you in starting an arbitration or mediation. On the site you will also find information about awards and a glossary of terms.

What Can You Expect?

About 40 percent of all claims never make it to the arbitration panel. In many cases the firm and the investor come to some kind of settlement prior to the arbitration date. There are also a large number of claims that the investor will simply withdraw without explanation.

Decisions on claims that go before the panel seem to run slightly in favor of the client. About 53 percent of the claims end with the client winning some or total satisfaction.

If you go to arbitration, will you need a lawyer? The answerer is a resounding "yes and no." There is no requirement for a lawyer. However, the broker-dealer will be represented by counsel who represents the firm in disputes and whose job it is to keep the firm's payments as low as possible. (His bonus is riding on it.) For that reason, investing in your own counsel is a good idea.

You (or your attorney) will submit two legal documents: a statement of claim and a case information sheet. FINRA will pass to each side the other side's information, along with additional materials about the arbitration system. The discovery process is streamlined, and depositions are very rare. Both sides may then ask for documents and a list of witnesses from the other side. Next, the arbitration hearing will be scheduled.

Both sides may call witnesses and give an opinion. Each side is allowed to examine and cross-examine the parties. In most cases, after the hearing is over, the three-member panel will step into another room to caucus. At that time, the panel will agree on the course of action that the parties should follow. They will return, announce their decision, and provide a written award form on the spot.

Mark stands and stretches. The room is quiet. The heavy dinner, the wine, and the long night have taken their toll.

"What's next month's topic?" asks Tim.

Bob replies, "How to make a business investment for maximum reward with minimum risk. And don't forget, I'm bringing whatever I catch on my fishing trip."

Part 3:

INVESTING MONEY AND TIME

14: Buying a Business

Good Opportunities Abound

The evening is warm, so as dinner approaches, we set up tables in the yard. Bob's fishing trip was a success. For dinner he makes a great salad and grilled fresh trout. The good food, along with the ample cold beer, helps the conversation around the table last so long that we almost don't get to our topic for the evening. When we realize the time, Mark quickly organizes us into a fire brigade line to move the dishes and glasses back to the kitchen. Bob stacks up everything to be washed in the morning, and we make our way onto the porch.

Tonight we plan to discuss how to buy a business. A decade ago, this topic might not have been included in a discussion of investing, but times have changed. Now, every month, several thousand people find themselves at a career crossroads. Maybe their employer went out of business or downsized. Maybe they became tired of working for someone else. In any event, many people decide that their future lies in running their own business.

Bob and Jack are the last two to join us. Bob, still standing and wiping his hands with a kitchen towel, speaks up. "You are right. I know three people, all my age, who have gone into business for themselves in the past year. It is no easy task, I can tell you. Who would have thought fifty-year-olds would be starting businesses in such large numbers?"

"Bob is right," I say. "The numbers are stunning. The National Franchise Association says that the fastest-growing segment of franchise buyers is comprised of people fifty to sixty-five years old."

If you are considering starting your own business, you have three options:

- Start a business from scratch.

- Buy an existing business.

- Buy a franchise.

The above are listed from highest to lowest in order of risk—and potential reward. When compared to other investment options reviewed in this book, starting a successful business from scratch stands head and shoulders above the rest for profit potential. However, it also far exceeds the others in terms of risk.

Not only do businesses started from scratch have the highest failure rate, they require the double-barreled investment of both your money and your time. If your new business fails, you not only lose your monetary investment, you also lose the two or three years you put into the venture. Money can be earned back, but the time is gone forever. I am *not* saying that no one should start a business from scratch. I have personally started at least half a dozen businesses. Some of them did very well, while others were disappointing. Whichever of the three options you're considering, be sure you approach the investment armed with as much information as possible.

There is no risk-free way to invest in your own business! However, you can take some important steps before committing your funds and time to a business project—steps that will dramatically improve your chances of success.

Tonight we will focus on two avenues to entering a business: franchising, and purchasing an existing business.

Franchises

The past ten years has seen an explosion in the number of new franchises being sold. Who is snapping them up? By far, the fastest growing group of buyers is people aged fifty and over. Instead of getting ready for retirement villages and shuffleboard, this segment of the population is busy launching new business ventures, and many of these are franchises.

You may have become acquainted with the concept of a franchise when you saw the first McDonald's go up in your neighborhood, but franchising has been around for a very long time. British businessmen used a form of franchising with colonial businesses even before the Revolutionary War. Benjamin Franklin used a type of franchise arrangement to expand his printing company. (Yes, *Poor Richard's Almanac* was a franchise.) Today, you can find franchising everywhere.

When most people think of franchising, they think of food service, and with good reason. You can franchise everything from a pretzel stand to Bennigan's Grill and Tavern (total cost, about $2 million). Franchising goes way beyond food, however. Want an automobile-related franchise? You could consider a Dent Doctor (total cost, about $75,000) or a Maaco Auto Paint Shop (total cost, about $250,000) or Payless Car Rental (total cost as high as $6 million), just to name a few options. Not interested in cars? No problem. There are franchise dating services, printing shops, carpet cleaners, and hair salons. Any industry you can name is likely to have franchise opportunities.

The Value Is in the Plan

Typically, new franchisees have a far greater chance of success than a person who starts a new business from scratch. Many experts point to instant name recognition of a franchise business as the source of this success, and I agree. However, the true value of the franchise lies in its business plan. A refined and tested business plan is worth its weight in gold. The business operation plan for a McDonald's lays out exactly what every employee should be doing, minute by minute. A Dunkin' Donuts franchisee knows exactly how much filling to squirt into each jelly doughnut, and a Roto-Rooter franchisee (total cost, about $50,000) has a set of newspaper and Yellow Pages ads that have proven to be successful. A tested business plan reduces your guesswork to zero (or as close to zero as possible).

Eventually, you would figure out for yourself how much jelly to use in your doughnuts or how many sets of golf clubs to stock at your Pro Golf Discount franchise (total cost, about $850,000), but when you buy a franchise you know these details on day one. In effect, when you buy a franchise, you benefit from the accumulated knowledge and experience of the businesspeople who have gone before you. A franchise is only as good as its business plan. If the plan is rock-solid and well tested, your probability of success improves.

The downside of owning a franchise is that it requires you to sacrifice much of your creativity for the uniformity of the system. If potential for success is what attracts you to a business, rather than the thought of doing everything your way, a franchise may be a good choice for you.

"I'm glad we're having this discussion," says Jack. "There's talk that the place where I work is going to be sold to a foreign buyer that will close the U.S. plant as soon as possible. Once that happens, I expect that the office staff will be pared back to just the sales group, which would leave me and seventy-five other people on the street. I must admit that I've been a little paralyzed by the thought of looking for a new job. I did look at buying a franchise, but it seems pretty overwhelming."

"Jack, you're not alone," I tell him. "This same story is repeated every day. Let's talk about how you should go about finding the right franchise."

Considering Your Options and Narrowing Your Search

When you start gathering information about available franchise opportunities, your first stop will be your local bookstore. *Entrepreneur Magazine* publishes a very good book titled the *Ultimate Book of Franchises*. Another good book is *The Franchise Bible*, also published by Entrepreneur Press.

The next stop is your computer. You can search the Internet for information on franchise opportunities. To save time, be as specific in your search as possible. Earlier today, when I Googled "franchise," I got 101,000,000 hits. Tomorrow there will be more.

When considering what type of franchise you might be interested in, ask yourself the following questions:

- What type of business most interests you?

- What do you enjoy doing with your time?

- What industries do you know best?

- How much are you hoping to earn?

- How much do you want to invest?

- Do you have a bigger strategy? (In other words, do you want to buy several franchises of the same type and cover a region?)

Once you have selected the industry where you would be happy spending your time and energy, your search becomes much easier. *Entrepreneur Magazine* provides a list of franchise opportunities arranged by industry. You also can attend a franchise show to review a large number of franchises in one place (as described in the next section on page 169).

I don't want to mislead anyone. Searching the Internet for the right franchise opportunity can be like hunting for a needle in a haystack, and walking a franchise show will get you 90 percent sore feet and only 10 percent usable information. But don't be discouraged. These exercises will be very important as you build a frame of reference for the opportunity you're seeking.

After you have narrowed your list, it's time to get into your car and visit a few operations. Act like a customer. Are you satisfied with the product or service? Are you comfortable with how the operation looks, feels, and functions? Be sure to visit the franchise at various times. An ice cream franchise may look promising on the hottest day of the year, but a return visit in cool or rainy weather will give you a more complete picture. If the franchise does not lend itself to a visit, you may need to phone and pretend to be a prospect. In any event, you should have firsthand experience doing business with the franchise as a customer before you seriously consider becoming a franchisee.

Attending a Franchise Show

Attending franchise shows is like trying to find gold in a minefield; the experience can be both wonderful and horrible.

What's so wonderful? Here are a few examples:

- In one place, in one day, you will be able to make personal contact with and obtain information from 50 to 250 different franchise organizations.

- You can set appointments to meet with franchise company representatives after the show to discuss their offerings in detail.

- Even if you learn very little at a franchise show, you will get lots to eat. Someone is always giving away something: a sample of great ice cream, coffee in tiny little cups, warm pretzels with toppings that drip all over your pants, and bags of fresh popcorn.

And why franchise shows are simultaneously horrible:

- Commissioned salespeople staff the booths. They may have little knowledge of the workings of the franchise beyond what they were told at the sales meeting the day before the show opened.

- Very few of the booths (assume none) will give out their full offering document, the uniform franchise offering circular (UFOC). The UFOC is the official offering document that every franchise must provide to each new franchisee. Think of it like a mutual fund prospectus. (See page 175 for a discussion of the UFOC's contents.) Without a copy of the UFOC, you have only spotty information, at best.

- The majority of the franchises offered at the show will be of no interest to you.

- Some of the best franchises do not work the show circuit.

With a little planning, you can avoid some of the downsides of franchise shows. Start by reviewing a list of the exhibitors ahead of time. You can generally find the list of expected exhibitors on the show's Web site, or you can grab a show directory when you arrive. In either case, go over the list and identify the exhibitors that interest you *before* you start walking the floor.

Get to the show early, and go straight to the exhibitors you want to visit. Have a prepared list of questions that are important to you, such as these:

- What can you tell me about your franchisee support or training program?

- What is the typical total cost of start-up?

- Do you require a minimum of business experience, and if so, what type?

- How long has the company been franchising?

- How many franchisees are in your system?

- What makes your franchise better than your competitors in the same industry?

- How do I get a copy of the "Uniform Franchise Offering Circular?

After you have spoken to the few franchises that are meaningful to you, walk over and get one of those free tiny little cups of coffee, find a place to sit down, and make notes of what you learned. If you are lucky, you will be out before the convention hall gets flooded with the 10,000 people who just want to wander around.

The First Meeting with the Company Sales Representative

By this time, you may have narrowed your list of potential franchise opportunities to just three or four candidates. Call the home office of your short-list franchisors, and ask to speak with the sales representative for your area. (The home office contact person's name, address, and phone number will be on the company Web site.)

Unlike those random meetings with representatives at a franchise show, this meeting will come after you have begun to research the company. You will have begun forming your opinion of the company, and you will have a new list of questions, such as:

- How long has the company been franchising, and how many outlets are operating? Many new franchise companies may charge lower fees. However, the older more mature companies tend to have more refined and proven programs.

- What are the company's minimum qualifications (both financial and experiential) for a franchise purchaser? The answer to this question is very important to you, and not just because you want to know if you qualify to own one of their franchises. The higher the qualifications bar, the more serious the company is about the success of its franchisees. If the company will sell a franchise to anyone who has the money (or can get the money, or who will sign a note for the money), it probably wants to earn as much in up-front fees as possible. The smart franchisor only wants to sell franchises to individuals who have a high probability of success. McDonald's, for example, accepts only one of every 120 applications it receives.

- What does the training program involve? How long is it, where is it held, is there an additional charge for the program, and what does it teach? Is the program relevant to your needs? (The training program for one health club chain focused primarily on how to open your bank account and make out the deposit slip—not very helpful.) Are there follow-up training programs or other programs for the franchisees?

- What type of company contact should you expect after the training program? Company contact is good. If you hear that the franchisor "pretty much leaves you alone once the business starts," take it as a warning sign that the franchisor has more interest in your start-up fee than in your long-term success. Further, if the franchisor representatives aren't visiting you, they probably aren't visiting other franchisees, either. When that happens, the quality at each outlet will start to vary, and the power of the franchise will be diminished.

- How strictly does the franchisor monitor franchisees' adherence to a set of standards? Every franchisee can suffer when the franchisor doesn't monitor and maintain a strict set of standards at every location. A customer who is turned off by the experience at one franchise location is unlikely to visit—or recommend to others—that franchise in any location. A few slackers in the system will reflect negatively on all the others.

It may be difficult, but do not jump into your questions at the beginning of the meeting. Instead, allow the representative to make his or her full presentation. Their presentation may provide you with new information and add to or improve your questions.

Reviewing Franchise Fees

Now for some of the most important questions you should ask the company representative—those that deal with how, exactly, the franchisor makes its money.

It is essential that you understand the answer to these questions. All fees should be clear and reasonable. Be vigilant. Some fees may raise a red flag about the franchisor's motives. Not only do you want to identify and fully understand the fees, you want to know exactly what services you will be getting for each fee you pay. Here are some of the questions you might ask to help better explore the issues of fees and costs:

- What up-front fees must you pay? Generally, the initial franchise fee is the down payment that you must pay to buy a franchise. Some franchise companies want the full amount up front. Others will accept a portion of the fee and finance the balance. (Be sure to check the interest rate as compared to the rate for business loans in your community.) Watch out for a franchise that will finance the balance due on its start-up fee but requires you to use its finance company. This may be a sign that the company is more interested in earning interest than in your long-term success. What about other up-front fees? Is there an extra charge for training? Is there a charge for signage?

- What ongoing fees must franchisees pay? These can include royalty fees, service fees, marketing and advertising charges, ongoing training fees, and sustaining or renewal fees, among others. Some franchisors charge an annual audit fee.

- What exclusive product costs are charged to franchisees? In many franchises, there is a product or method that is exclusive to that organization, and franchisees are required to buy the product from the franchisor. For example, you would expect that if you buy a Baskin-Robbins Ice Cream franchise (total cost, about $400,000 to $500,000), you will be required to serve only Baskin-Robbins ice cream. If you buy a Sylvan Learning Center franchise (about $200,000 start-up cost) you can expect to be required to buy and use Sylvan teaching supplies.

- Does the franchisor require that you buy common products from an exclusive source? In the operation of your business, you will use countless items that are not unique to a specific franchise, such as the phone system or the furniture in your office. If the franchisor requires that you buy these items from an exclusive provider, be sure to determine if the price charged for those items is reasonable.

- Must you rent the location from the franchisor? As with the previous item, if this is the case, you want to be sure the rent is a reasonable market rate.

- What other fees can franchisees expect to pay? Many franchisors charge a transfer fee if you sell or transfer your business to another person.

As a potential franchisee you must understand that the franchisor is in business to make a profit. And that as a practical matter, you will be the source of their profit. It is your responsibility to examine each fee to be sure that you will not be overburdened by unreasonable costs.

Talking to Other Franchisees

I cannot overemphasize the importance of speaking with two or more franchisees before you buy into a franchise. When you are weighing the decision to buy a franchise, your attorney and your CPA can help you to a point. However, only someone who is living the business every day can tell you what you *really* need to know before you jump in.

The franchise salesperson will be happy to give you a list of franchisees and suggest that you call them. I recommend that you ignore such lists. You can expect that the salesperson will point you toward only the most successful or franchisor-friendly people in the system. Instead, strike out on your own to find and contact other franchisees. (In my experience, most are very forthcoming, honest, and helpful.) Before your meeting, make up a list of questions such as these:

- Are you happy that you bought this franchise?

- The salesperson said that most franchisees have an annual gross revenue of $XYZ. Is that amount realistic?

- What about margins?

- Is the franchisee start-up training and ongoing training valuable?

- What are the biggest challenges I should plan for (hiring, seasonality, employee theft, and so on)?

- Is there anything you wish you had known before you started?

- Have you had any negative surprises since starting the business?

- Do you think that the franchisor is responsive to the franchisees?

- Do you have much contact with other franchisees?

- Could you give me the name of another franchisee you think I should speak with?

Don't stop after talking to just one franchisee. Remember that the knowledge and understanding of the existing franchisees is more valid than anything the salesperson or franchisor literature will say.

The Uniform Franchise Offering Circular (UFOC)

The U.S. Federal Trade Commission requires every franchisor to provide to potential franchisees a legal document called a uniform franchise offering circular (UFOC). The document is designed to help you compare franchise offerings. True to its name, the UFOC includes mandatory sections, laid out in uniform order. You will already have discussed some of this information in your meeting with the sales rep, but read this document carefully. Take special note of projected fees and the franchisor's obligations to you as a franchisee. The contents of this document are much more important to your future than are the salesperson's promises. The required sections in the UFOC include the following:

- An overview of the franchisor and any predecessor company

- The franchisor's business experience (generally the past five years)

- Litigation history for the past ten years

- A listing of any bankruptcies declared by the franchisor in the past ten years

- Initial fees

- Ongoing and other fees

- Projected total initial investment

- Restrictions on source of product

- Franchisee obligations

- Information as to any financing that the franchisor may offer

- The franchisor's obligations (what the franchisor will do for you)

- Territory protection (if any)

- Trademarks, patents, copyrights, and proprietary information

- Time obligation, for instance, whether the franchisor requires you to be an on-site business operator

- Restrictions on what you may sell: If you just bought a Seattle Sutton's Healthy Eating franchise—total cost about $500,000—don't expect they will allow you to add your sister's mile-high chocolate cake to the menu. On the other hand, some franchisors allow you to carry other products that are "noncompetitive" or complementary to their line.

- The provisions and rules for selling or transferring your franchise

- The provisions and guidelines for dispute resolution

- Public figure involvement: Some franchise companies use public figures in their endorsements or in their advertising to attract new franchisees. Some franchises even use the name of a well-known person in the name of the company. An example is Arthur Treacher's Fish & Chips—total cost about $220,000. The UFOC should explain that Arthur Treacher really has nothing to do with the day-to-day business. You might have suspected that, since Mr. Treacher passed away in 1975.

- Earnings claims: This information is essentially voluntary and unverified, so take it with a grain of salt. The FTC doesn't check its accuracy, nor does any state regulatory agency. Because earnings projections in the UFOC could end up as lawsuit fodder for a dissatisfied franchisee, the vast majority of franchisors just leave out an earnings projection section.

- List of outlets: This is frequently a separate attachment that lists any company-owned outlets and current franchises. This section also must include a list of any franchisees that have left the system in the past year. The list of recently departed franchisees is very interesting because this group may have opinions about the company that you would like to know before you sign on the dotted line. The franchisor must also supply you with the contact information for these ex-franchisees.

- The franchisor's financial statements: Read them. Work only with a financially secure franchisor.

- A sample franchisee/franchisor contract

Covering the Bases

Here are a few final words of advice for those interested in buying a franchise:

- When searching for the right franchise opportunity, you may need to do some detective work. The best franchises often do not advertise in magazines or set up a booth at the local franchise show. You must seek them out.

- Any deadline is your deadline, not the salesperson's (whose pay may come solely from commissions). You may hear, "You better grab it now or the territory that you want will be gone." Or, "You need to sign the contract before the end of the month because the fees may be going up." No matter what the salesperson says, this is your deal, your money, and your livelihood. Make your decisions at your pace.

- Talk to everyone, but listen most closely to the existing franchise holders (those you find, not the ones from the list the salesperson gave to you).

- Hire an attorney with experience in franchising to help you with contracts and to provide general counsel during the process.

Finally, remember that you can walk away from the negotiation at any time. There are thousands (really, thousands) of available franchises. Be willing to take the time to find the one that is right for you.

"Jack, did we cover some elements that could make a franchise search more productive?" I ask.

"We sure did. However, there is another piece to the puzzle that I am dealing with. Remember the first time we got together, I said that I was also considering buying an existing business?"

"Sure, I do, I think you said it was a printing company near the airport," I respond.

"Yes, that's it. Now I feel better about knowing what to look for in a franchise. If I still want to consider an existing business, is there a similar set of guidelines I can follow?" asks Jack.

Buying a Business

Buying a successful business offers many advantages over starting a business from scratch, but it also carries some disadvantages. You need to consider both when weighing your decision to invest in an existing business.

Here are some of the advantages:

- The business is operating and, we will assume, generating positive cash flow.

- The business has identified its customers, and some of those customers are loyal to the business.

- Key employees are in place.

- Inventory is in place, along with a list of reliable suppliers (suppliers are more willing to give terms to existing businesses).

- Unreliable suppliers have been weeded out.

- Business systems, such as accounting and payroll, are in place.

- It is much easier to obtain financing from a lender.

Here are some disadvantages:

- You may pay a premium for an established business as opposed to starting one from scratch.

- Employees can be difficult during transition.

- You may be buying obsolete inventory, equipment, or systems.

- The business may have out-of-date processes and procedures.

- Some of the accounts receivable that you bought with the business may be difficult to collect.

Being a Wise Shopper

When shopping for an existing business, you have to make some basic, yet critical, decisions. The first of these involves how you go about conducting your search. Unfortunately, many people waste a lot of time and energy by failing to undertake this step in a productive manner. These people tend to begin their search by reading the "Businesses for Sale" section in the paper or by calling business brokers and asking, "What's for sale?" That approach can lead you down too many dead ends and may cause you to end up with a business for which you have little affinity.

Instead, begin by making up a checklist. If you read the earlier sections on buying a franchise, you have seen this list before:

- What type of business most interests you?

- What do you enjoy doing with your time?

- What industries do you know best?

- How much are you hoping to earn?

- How much do you want to invest?

- Is there a bigger strategy? (In other words, do you want to buy several companies in the same industry?)

After you have answered these questions, you will have a better understanding of what you are looking for, and you will be better able to communicate your interests. That means you will improve the results of your search. You can eliminate some businesses or industries from your search and use your time more productively.

Following Leads and Asking the Right Questions

When you have selected the industry that you would like to be in, avenues for finding your candidate will open up. For example, the industry you have chosen will most likely have a professional association. Join it. The association's newsletter, Web site, and meetings can be a great source of prospective candidates. You can also contact suppliers and ask if they know anyone who may be thinking of selling. Ask your banker, lawyer, or CPA if they have a client in the industry to whom they could introduce you. Those contacts may know of companies available for sale. When seeking leads from a business broker or an industry professional, remember to be clear and precise as to what you are looking for. You don't need to spend your time visiting a $20 million business if you have a $200,000 budget.

When you learn of a business for sale, be sure to find out why the seller is selling it. Don't assume that a problem with the business is prompting the sale. Excellent businesses go up for sale every day. Many completely rational reasons can prompt an owner to sell a perfectly good business:

- Seller's age/retirement
- Seller's health or the health of a family member
- Divorce—the need to split up assets
- Relocation to a new area
- Other business interests

Here's one helpful hint: You want to establish if the business owner is ready to sell when you are ready to buy. Spending your time with a seller who is just testing the waters is a waste of your valuable time.

Sadly, the only device we have for establishing a seller's level of commitment to a sale is the question, "Why are you selling?"

Because this is your only tool, use it carefully. Ask the question, and listen closely to the answer. I have found that if a person cannot give a clear and logical reason for the sale in one sentence, he probably is on a fishing trip and is hoping that you will be the fish.

The Importance of Due Diligence

Due diligence is the careful review and verification of each business fact presented by the seller. It is almost impossible to conduct due diligence properly without the help of professionals. Your CPA and attorney are essential in this process. They (and you) will want to verify these things:

- Inventory
- Bank balances
- Balance sheet

- Income statements
- Revenue claims
- Accounts receivable
- Accounts payable
- Old tax returns
- Taxes and permits due
- Outstanding legal claims and any history of litigation
- Liens
- Union and employee actions
- Pension obligations
- Product guarantees for previously sold items
- New or pending regulations that may have an adverse effect
- Zoning changes
- Product liability
- New or changing competition

You should even check to see if the city (or county) is planning nearby road construction that could affect the business.

Checking Out the Seller—and the Books

Try to determine the reputation of the business and its owner. If the seller has a poor reputation for service, quality, or honesty, you will be buying that bad reputation along with the business assets.

Also check to see if the seller has sold this or another business in the past. Talk to the buyers. I know a person who sold his business four different times. Each time the buyer had "unexpected difficulties," and each time the old owner got the business back for no money. (Would you want to be buyer number five? I wouldn't.)

As you conduct due diligence, remember that some sellers are unscrupulous. They will puff up or cook their books to make the business appear more successful than it really is. Many business buyers have been disappointed when they realize they have been taken in by a set of cooked books. To avoid that, ask your CPA if the company's numbers align with industry standards.

If the typical company in this industry has an inventory turnover rate of five times a year, and this business is claiming a turn rate of nine times a year, you need to investigate. If most businesses in this industry have a gross margin of 40 percent and this company is claiming 55 percent, you need to investigate. If the typical store in this industry grosses $300 a square foot, and this company claims $500 a square foot, investigate. You get the picture.

If you find that the seller has inflated the company's earnings or inventory by puffing the books, you can point it out and seek a correction, or you can just walk away. I suggest the latter. If the seller lied about this, he has probably told other lies that you haven't discovered yet.

As you talk with the seller, he is likely to say a lot of positive things about the business. You will come to rely upon many of these claims. That is only natural. Your goal should be to turn those comments and claims into warranties. Make note of all of the important claims your seller presents during your conversations. Prior to closing, repeat them back to the seller and tell him that you want to put them in the purchase agreement. If you do so, and the information turns out to be false, you may be able to obtain damages from the seller. Your attorney is critical in the proper execution of this process.

Understanding the Sales Process

The lifeblood of every business is sales. Your due diligence review must include a complete understanding of the company's sales process. Here are just a few points that you will want to check:

- Is the market for the product or service growing, stagnating, or declining?

- Are the company's sales driven by the owner's personal efforts? How will that person's departure affect future sales?

- Is there one superstar salesperson, and if so, how will you deal with that person?

- How many customers is the company serving? Would the departure of just one large customer spell financial difficulty?

- Does your purchase date need to be scheduled around seasonal sales? (If May is the busiest month, for example, you don't want to buy in June or July and then have to wait a full year to generate meaningful revenue.)

- Have sales grown in the past year? Was the increase because of price-cutting that may not be sustainable?

- Is a new competitor about to invade the territory?

- Is there a business or billing cycle you should know about?

- What about the cycle of costs? Is a major cost coming due shortly?

In addition to these questions, ask if you can go on a sales call or somehow observe the sales process. Your firsthand experience will offer valuable insights.

Valuing a Company

How do you value a company that you are considering? Generally, you will base your offering price on one of three computation methods:

- Comparables

- Net assets

- Future positive cash flow

The comparables method of valuation is relatively straightforward. If the business is one of many in its industry, there may have been other sales before this transaction. If businesses with a similar profile are bought and sold regularly, there will be a trail of valuation information upon which you can determine a reasonable price offer. Your CPA or business broker can be very helpful when researching comparable sales data.

The remaining two methods require a bit more explanation.

Using Net Assets to Value a Business

The net assets method of valuation requires that you value the business assets. That takes a bit of work.

First, consider the value you would assign to the business inventory. Remember to give this a critical review, as some of the inventory may be obsolete or out of style and thus of lower value.

Next, you can value the company's equipment by comparing each piece of equipment on hand to similar items in the used-equipment market.

Next, if you are buying the accounts receivable, be sure to discount their face value. If you would like a formula to help compute the amount of discount that you offer when buying account receivables see my Web site. Go to *www.dennisblitz.com* and click on "Book Supplement."

Using the Cash Flow Method of Valuation

Many believe this to be the most reasonable method of valuing a business. After all, why are you buying a business? It's not because you have a desire to own inventory; it is because you want the positive cash flow. The following is one of many formulas for determining cash flow.

Suppose the business has an annual positive cash flow of $1 million. You are interested in buying and running the business. You believe that your time is worth $150,000 a year. After deducting that amount, there will be an excess positive cash flow of $850,000. Let's say that you are seeking a 15 percent return on your investment. In that case, the value of the business would be $5,666,667 ($850,000 divided by 0.15). If you are seeking a 17.5 percent return, the value would be $4,857,143 ($850,000 divided by 0.175).

This is a very simplified example and is described here as a framework for valuation, not as a rule. A good CPA will have other methods of valuation you can consider.

Stock or Asset Purchase

Talk with an attorney to determine whether you should buy the stock of the company or its assets. Frequently, there are advantages to buying the assets of a business—its inventory, fixtures, company name, and so on—rather than buying the business itself. For example, the business may have liabilities that the owner failed to disclose or simply forgot. When you buy the stock of a business, you are buying everything (including its liabilities). However, if you buy only the business assets, you may have an additional layer of separation between yourself and the former owner's liability.

Structuring and Finalizing the Deal

Setting the price is only half the story of a business sale; the rest is the structure or terms of the deal. Resist paying the full price on the day of closing. Be aggressive in trying to hold back as much of the purchase price as possible. Keeping your down payment small will give you extra funds to use during the transition period. It also helps to make the seller more interested in your success and thus more likely to be helpful. Many sellers of small businesses are perfectly happy to accept a lower down payment. They consider your future installment payments as a supplement to their retirement income.

Here are a few other factors to consider when finalizing the deal:

- Right of offset: Ask your attorney about adding a right-of-offset provision to the purchase agreement. If you experience a future loss due to a misstatement or misrepresentation by the seller, you may be able to offset, or deduct, the amount of the damages from payments still due the seller.

- Learning curve: Decide how much training or guidance you need so that you will be able to operate the business properly. Talk with the seller about his/her willingness to coach you after the closing. It is a good idea to clarify this transition training in the purchase agreement.

- Hold-over employees: Be sure to talk with the staff. Remember they will be anxious about your plans and intentions. Spending time with them is the best way to answer their concerns.

"This has been helpful; I think I have writer's cramp from taking so many notes," says Jack.

"Which sounds more appealing to you: buying a franchise or buying an existing business?" I ask.

"Of course, I really need to look over the franchising opportunities, but I must admit that I like that printing company that I mentioned last month, and I have about a hundred ideas for changes that could make that company so much better," answers Jack.

"Slow down a minute. If you do buy that printing company, you may want to consider a traditional transition pattern," I suggest to Jack.

"There is a traditional transition pattern?" responds Jack with a surprised look on his face.

"There sure is," I say.

Taking Charge

"Jack, let's say that it's Monday morning. You just closed the deal, and you want to remake the business in your vision. My best advice is don't do anything. Don't rush in and change the pricing or the packaging or the employee wage rate or size of the staff."

If the business is operating profitably, you might set up the following schedule for implementing change:

Days 1 to 30: Actively listen to everyone who wants to tell you what needs to be changed and what needs to stay. Listen carefully but make no promises.

Days 31 to 60: Ask questions—lots of questions. Touch, feel, and taste as much as possible. Try to understand every aspect and phase of the business.

Days 61 to 90: Take the time to fully develop your plan.

Day 91: Put your plan in action.

At first blush, you might think that the Nine Rules of Successful Investing don't apply when buying a business or franchise. However, they are just as relevant as with every other investment decision. Let's take a look:

1. Invest in what you know. Do not invest in a business if you do not have knowledge of that industry.

2. Invest, succeed, repeat. Identify those business practices that are profitable and repeat, repeat, repeat.

3. Embrace the learning curve. Ask a lot of questions before you put down your money, and keep learning every day you own the business.

4. Avoid losing money. The best way to do this is to buy an existing successful business or invest in a proven franchise.

5. Create a complementary combination of investments. All business has risk, so you may want to shift some of your other assets to fixed investments.

6. Take charge of one investment. There's no better way than to run your own business.

7. Keep it simple. Make this your guide every step of the way. With each choice or option, try to select the least complex action.

8. Trust your method. In this case, your business plan is your method. Remember, a proven business plan is the greatest value that franchising provides.

9. Rebalance your portfolio. Always take at least some of your earnings out of the business. Too many people reinvest every nickel in the business, which leaves them with an unbalanced portfolio of investments.

Starting a business or franchise can be a lot of work. It requires an investment of time, money—and a leap of faith. In the end, however, running your own business can offer generous rewards and provide an asset that you can sell when you are ready to retire.

This has been a long night, and we've covered a lot of ground. We could go on talking about each of these topics for hours more, but as the old saying goes, "The mind can only absorb as long as the seat can endure." I for one have come to my limit.

Notepads start to close. Bob stretches while still in his chair, and Tim is busy writing a last few notes. Carol asks Jack, "Exactly where is that printing company located?"

I walk over to Mark. "Mark, I need to leave early in the morning. Here are the keys; can you lock up for me after everyone leaves?"

"No problem," says Mark. "A couple of us are going out for breakfast before heading back to the city. Sure you can't stay?"

"I'd like to, but I'm meeting a guy who has a piece of land that I may want to buy," I tell Mark. "See you next month."

15: You and Real Estate

Donald Trump, Get Out of the Way!

It began raining early in the morning and hasn't let up. A little after lunch, almost everyone has arrived. One by one, each person makes their way out to the porch. I notice that most are carrying folders or notebooks. Bob is even carrying a rather thick brief case.

Lou quickly gains everyone's attention. "Since we began our visits, I have completely changed the way I look at my investments," he says. Laughing, he continues, "Actually, before we started having these talks, I almost never checked on my investments. I just bought a few stocks here and there and hoped for the best. Anyway, I was holding a couple of mutual funds that I realized were averaging less than market return and several stocks that I bought on tips but had gone nowhere since I picked them up. It was almost like I was holding dead money.

"First, I sold all of the funds and stocks, and then I did exactly what we talked about. I decided that the natural resource and tech stock sectors both offered good growth opportunities. Then, using a filter on my broker's Web site, I found the five fastest-growing companies in each sector. Last, I looked up the insider-trading information and picked the two stocks in each sector that showed an increase in insider buying. Those are the stocks I bought. My investment has gone up about 5 percent in the past six weeks."

Suddenly, everyone wanted to talk. Jack goes next. "When I got home, I wrote down all of my investments and discovered that I was almost 90 percent invested in Vanguard's S&P 500 Fund. It hit me like a brick: This is really poor planning! Almost everything I have is bet on one horse.

"I know that I want to place some money in real estate and I also wanted to experiment with writing covered calls. When we talked about covered calls in July it sounded so easy that I tried it. When I went to actually make the trade, I was in a state of panic. What if I did something wrong? What if I hit the wrong key on my computer? What if . . . ? Well, you get the idea.

"So I called the online broker, gave him my account number, and said I wanted to write a covered call using some stock I had bought the day before. I asked if he could walk me through the process. In two minutes, he had me transferred to some guy in his options trading department who was very knowledgeable and patient. I put on the trade and learned a lot as he took me by the hand, step by step. I also learned that you can buy your underlying stock and write the option in a single trade. It's called a buy-write, and because it is a single trade, the commission is lower than if you did it as two separate transactions."

The afternoon goes on that way, with each person telling her or his experience and sharing useful information with the others. Before we know it, it's dinnertime. Anne comes into the room to tell us that she has set up everything buffet style in the kitchen. She suggests that we help ourselves to dinner and bring everything back to the porch.

The conversations race on as we enjoy dinner. The moment we finish eating, I notice that Bob has reached into his briefcase and withdrawn a thick paperback. Furiously turning pages, he finally looks up and asks, "Does anyone know how many points it is for mushroom soup?"

Half the room laughs. The other half (the thin people) don't get it.

Anne asks, "Did you have a cup or a bowl?"

"A cup."

"Oh. I don't know. Put down three points," she replies.

"Say, we need to get going. Real estate is a broad topic," I say.

When putting together a diversified portfolio, having a portion of your funds invested in real estate makes good sense. You can use two strategies for investing in real estate:

- Buy it and hold it. Simply put, this strategy results in a real estate investment in which you own property and earn money from its rental. Your real estate asset might be a single-family residence, a duplex, a four-flat, or a seventy-story office building. You may have invested in a small strip mall, an industrial building, or even the land on which someone else has developed a project.

- Buy it, fix it up, and sell it. When you use this strategy, your real estate earnings come from transactions. Real estate transactions aren't true investments. Instead, they represent a business in which the merchandise being sold happens to be property.

No matter which of these strategies you pursue, real estate investments are a classic choice for growing your assets.

What Kind of Investor Are You?

When investing in real estate you can choose to be an active or a passive investor.

The active investor is a hands-on person who takes responsibility for the project. If you are an active real estate investor, you will locate and develop the property yourself, then maintain or sell it.

The passive real estate investor invests through a limited partnership (LP) or real estate investment trust (REIT). Investors in LPs and REITs are free from any day-to-day activity or responsibility. LPs and REITs are discussed further on page 201. For now, just be aware that both Limited Partnerships and REITs carry fees associated with someone else doing the work on your behalf.

Is the Time Right to Buy?

Newly minted real estate investors always ask the same question: "When is the best time to invest in real estate?"

Here is the simple answer: The best time to buy real estate was in the 1950s. Anyone who bought a property then and still holds it today is sitting on sixty years of appreciation.

Of course, many people didn't buy real estate in the 1950s because prices were too high. The high prices were understandable. The economy was booming as 1.6 million solders returned home from World War II and started families. The demand for new homes pushed real estate prices out of sight.

So, I guess that the best time to buy was the 1960s.

Yet, in the 1960s the price of real estate was high. The baby boom was at its peak. Shopping malls were busy, landlords were able to charge ever-increasing rent rates. No, prices for real estate were too high in the 1960s.

Of course there were ample excuses for not buying real estate in the 1970s, 1980s and 1990s.

Okay, forget the past. We're in the first decade of the 2000s. Is this a good time to invest in real estate? Again, prices for real estate are high, but remember that we considered the prices high every decade for the past sixty years.

Most people understand that real estate prices tend to increase in the long term. Yet, the nagging question remains. Has the ideal time to invest in real estate passed me by; is it *too late for me to start*?

The answer to this concern goes all the way back to our earliest discussions. For the vast majority of would-be investors, the "it's too late for me" mindset is simply wrong. Due to today's longer life expectancy, you might be twenty investment years younger than you realize. This gives you an extra twenty years for your investments to mature. Most investors have ample time for real estate appreciation to kick in.

Going with the Flow of Real Estate Cycles

Real estate investing can make a person wealthy, or it can be disastrous. Most of the time, the results are somewhere in between. Between the years 2000 to 2006, the U.S. economy enjoyed six consecutive years of significant growth in real estate values. The surge of interest in real estate as an investment was triggered by:

- Discomfort with investing in the stock market (Remember the tech stock bubble?)
- New investors with time to invest due to a career change
- The lure of profits
- Amnesia

"Amnesia?" says Carol.

"You betcha!" I reply. "Thousands of new investors completely forgot that real estate cycles are a fact of life. They completely erased from their memory the period of 1988 through 1992, when prices flattened and then declined, when properties stayed on the market for twelve, eighteen, and twenty-four months. Just as with other investments, the cycles in real estate repeat because people overcompensate with their investment dollars. When times are good, they invest too much, and when times are bad, they invest too little."

Even the pros suffer from this ailment. During the red-hot economy that ran from the beginning through the latter half of the 1980s, the Marriott Corporation went on a building rampage. In fewer than ten years, Marriott expanded its number of hotel rooms by a whopping sixfold. The company did this by finding land, building a hotel on it, and selling that hotel to an investor group while retaining a management agreement—they repeating the process multiple times. When the economy slowed in the late 1980s, Marriott was unprepared. By 1991, the company had $1.5 billion of debt on its books for hotels it had built but could not sell. Investors in some of the earlier deals were unhappy and began suing the company at the very time that revenues from management contracts were declining. Today, Marriott is doing well again, but the journey back took almost a decade.

Earning Money in Real Estate

How can you earn money from real estate? To quote Elizabeth Barrett Browning, "Let me count the ways." No other investment category can be successfully approached from so many directions. Choosing from among the various profit opportunities available to you will be a key to your success. Just remember the Nine Rules of Successful Investing, especially Rule Seven, "Keep It Simple." Real estate investors can do that by keeping their focus narrow. A narrow focus allows you to polish your skills and knowledge within a clearly defined area, thereby improving the reliability of your success. Having a narrow focus also sets you up to follow Rule Two, "Invest, Succeed, Repeat."

There are many ways to profit from real estate. Here are just a few of the opportunities:

Real Estate Investment	Profit Opportunities
Undeveloped land	Rent it to an agricultural company to be used for farming.
	Rent it to a business such as a drive-in movie theater.
	Plant Christmas trees for harvest.
	Rezone it for development and sell it by the piece.
	Develop it with roads and sewers and sell in lots.
	Hold it for future sale.
Residential property	Build and rent.
	Build and sell.
	Buy, fix, and sell.
	Buy and rent.
	Buy and convert to condos.
Commercial property	Lease as retail space.
	Develop as a shopping mall.
	Build warehouses.
	Build and lease office space.
	Build hotels.
	Build and sell or lease manufacturing space.
	Redevelop the land.
	Turn it into parking space.
	Develop as a golf course.

I look up and notice that Jack is off in his own world. "Jack," I say, "are you with us?"

"Not really," he says. "I don't even know why I came tonight. I have no experience with construction or any of the other elements that you need to understand if you hope to earn money in real estate. I know I can hire out this work, but to be honest, I don't even like dealing with tradespeople. Sure, I'd like to earn money in the real estate field. I just don't see that happening."

"Jack, I am really glad you brought up that point. Here is something that we all need to keep in mind regarding real estate. The field is very broad. There are all manner of opportunities for people with all types of skills. For example, you can take advantage of the excellent earning potential of real estate even if you never lift a hammer or deal with a city building inspector. Almost every real estate transaction is financed. Offering or arranging financing is an excellent way to earn good and reasonably safe returns from real estate."

"The financial side of the transaction is much more appealing to me than the property side. What are the profit opportunities of real estate financing?" asks Jack.

Here are a few:

1. Lend money to developers.

2. Lend money for a first mortgage.

3. Lend money for a second or third mortgage.

4. Offer bridge loans to people who need a fast down payment for a new home but haven't sold their current home.

5. Make home improvement loans.

6. Invest in triple-net leases. (A lease that requires the tenant to pay the cost of maintenance, insurance, and taxes for the leased property.)

"Last month I mentioned that I have made loans to individuals and that I would write down my simple criteria. Here's what I look for," I say while handing out a photocopy page to everyone. The page lists just six simple guidelines:

- I make a loan only when I can have real estate as collateral.

- I will only be the first lender, called the "first lien."

- I only loan up to 65 percent of the appraised value of the property.

- I keep the loan period short, generally twelve to eighteen months.

- I never loan money to friends.

- I always ask a real estate attorney to review all the documentation.

There is money to be made in real estate even when things do not go well. For instance, you can buy tax liens on properties with delinquent taxes due. (Earnings can run as high as 18 to 24 percent annually.) You can also buy and sell foreclosures. To many people, the idea of working with foreclosures sounds heartless. However, you don't need to be a predator; in fact, your financial involvement can help people who might otherwise lose their home.

"So, Jack, you can see what we mean about the breadth of possibilities. We've just listed thirty different avenues to earning a profit from a real estate investment, and these are just a few of the opportunities in this field. Becoming proficient in just one focused area can offer generous returns," I say.

Weighing the Pros and Cons

Let's slow down and be a bit deliberate before we dive headfirst into a real estate investment. Real estate investing carries a few challenges not found in other areas of investing:

- Exit strategy: Every investment must have an exit strategy, and in this area, real estate is among the most unreliable. Unlike stock, there is no ready market for real estate. Your ninety-five-unit apartment building may be a real cherry, but selling it could take a year, and selling only a part of it would be enormously complex.

- Financing: Unlike many other investments, almost every real estate investment requires financing. Financing adds cost and can complicate your project. The complexity of financing a real estate project becomes most apparent if something goes wrong and the lender begins placing additional restrictions on your activity.

- Ownership: Owning real estate has extra complexities, including insurance, tenant issues, late rent, vacancies, vandalism, maintenance, evictions, and so on.

It's true that when you invest in real estate, you always have the property should something go wrong, and yes, the real estate market does seem to always come back. However, the comeback may take a while. Before you make any real estate investment, ask yourself this *critical* question: "If it becomes necessary, can I afford to hold the investment until the market comes back?"

Investors who fail to consider this question run the risk of overextending themselves and may find that they are forced to sell their property under unfavorable conditions.

Still undecided? Let's list five reasons why this is an awful time to invest in real estate and five reasons why the best time to start is now. Here goes:

Five Reasons to Jump In Now

- Population growth, immigration, and the coming of age of the echo boomers (people born between 1976 and 1994, made up mostly of the children of the baby boomer generation) all represent potential renters or buyers for your real estate.

- Growth in the number of second-home buyers will increase the demand for your real estate product.

- Increasing incomes make renting or selling your project easier.

- There will be an ever-increasing pool of real estate investors who will bid up the value of your property in the future.

- New construction is not keeping up with new demand, hence, rents will rise. Large projects are becoming more difficult to develop due to increasing raw material costs, land use restrictions, and scarcity of space in prime locations.

Five Reasons to Stay Out of Real Estate for Now

- Tightened lending restrictions will dampen demand for your investment property when you are ready to sell.

- Real estate prices have increased faster than rents, thus reducing the percentage of return on investment.

- Of those people who are qualified homebuyers, 69 percent already own a home. This is the highest percent in history, and 2.5 percent higher than just five years ago.

- People's finances are stretched thin. U.S. homeowners now have less then 56 percent equity in their homes, the lowest percentage since 1953.

- Shifting credit requirements and a possible glut of inventory left over from the building boom that started in 2001 means that your property could be more difficult to sell.

What should you do? Should you invest in real estate? Should you invest a little or a lot? Should you buy now or wait? Once again, we can look back to the Nine Rules of Successful Investing. In particular, we'll find some guidance from Rule Five, "Create a Complementary Combination of Investments."

Real estate is complementary to almost every other investment class that we have discussed. Also, Rule Six, "Take Charge of One Investment," is helpful. For many people, real estate investing is a perfect retirement career.

If you understand these rules to say that most investors should consider having a part of their capital invested in real estate, give yourself a pat on the back. You have entered the path to long-term financial success.

Taking the First Step

Everyone has a story about an uncle who slowly accumulated real estate throughout his life and then was able to rely on the rental income to support a comfortable retirement. Many of us know someone who bought a property for a song, held it for twenty years (earning rent every month), and then sold it for a small fortune. Others have heard about the person who bought a property and was offered a 50 percent or even a 100 percent profit just a few months later. Here is something that you can be sure of about each of these three investors: They are no smarter than you. They just took the first step.

Before entering the world of real estate investing the new investor must narrow their focus. Here are six steps to accomplish that:

1. Decide how you want to participate in the real estate industry. Do you want to work with the asset itself or the financing of the asset?

2. Decide if you're interested in residential or commercial real estate.

3. Decide what you want to do. Do you see yourself as the developer, or the redeveloper, or are you a buy it-and-rent it investor?

4. Decide on a location. Most people invest close to where they live, but that may not be necessary for you.

5. Get started. Talk to professionals and people who are active in the field. Don't forget to talk with your lawyer and CPA about your plans.

6. Plan to start small. Remember, your first few deals are learning opportunities. Make your mistakes on the little deals, not the big ones.

One final note about being a real estate investor: Plan to allocate adequate time to this process. Real estate transactions are deceptively time-consuming. Real estate investment opportunities require time to find, negotiate, close, develop, rent, or sell. Even if you plan to be a hands-on investor, you may find that you must depend on others to complete some of the work, and sometimes those people may not have your sense of urgency.

If you want to invest in real estate but are concerned that time will be an obstacle, don't fret; what comes next will address that exact concern. "Now, where did I put my coffee cup?" I ask.

16: Investing in Real Estate from Your Armchair

I Don't Have the Time; I Just Want the Money

Carol turns to a fresh page on her notepad. "This is for me," she says. "I have some long-term stocks that I am holding, and so far I'm doing nicely with the covered-call options that I have been writing. But I need an investment to complement these two, and real estate is going to be it. However, I just do not have the time to invest directly."

"There are two important difficulties that real estate investors face," I respond. "First, real estate investing can be very time-consuming. Next, because of the large amounts of leverage common to most real estate deals, these investments can be risky. Leverage is wonderful when things go the right way. However, if a project runs late, sells slowly, or fails to rent, the persistent tick-tock of the monthly interest payments can extract a heavy toll."

These two stumbling blocks have kept many people from investing in real estate. Worry not. The free enterprise system has provided us with solutions (for a price, of course). The solutions are real estate partnerships and real estate investment trusts (REITs). Let's begin with partnerships.

Should You Invest in a Partnership?

If you would like to have real estate in your portfolio, but you want to share the risks and responsibilities of ownership and management, you may consider investing in a partnership. Real estate partnerships come in two forms, general partnerships and limited partnerships

General Partnerships

A general partnership gives you an opportunity to join forces with others who have assets or skills that complement your own. Your partners may have contacts or experience that you lack. In a partnership, two or more people can share the workload, and each can bring ideas and concepts to the project. Just as balance is essential to a successful investment portfolio, a partnership gives you the opportunity to balance your skills while sharing responsibilities and liabilities—and yes, the profits—with your partners.

Partnerships are not all blue skies and daffodils, and a general partnership carries a critical downside. By definition, each partner in a general partnership has unlimited liability. That means that you can be held responsible not just for your own financial mistakes but for those of your partners, as well. A first-time match-up can be a stressful experience. In the worst-case scenario, you could find yourself in a situation where dealing with your partners becomes more complex than the project itself.

Limited Liability Partnerships

Generally called a limited partnership, this is a partnership in which only one partner is required to accept the responsibility of unlimited liability. The person or people who accept that risk then become the general partners; all others are referred to as limited partners. Each limited partner has at risk only the amount that she or he originally agreed to and no more. To maintain their limited liability status, limited partners also are limited in their authority. Only the general partners can make policy decisions.

By the time the investors are offered a limited partnership investment, the general partners likely have been working on the project for six, twelve, or even eighteen months. In that time, they will have done the following:

Located the site or project

Secured the site

Checked local regulations and restrictions

Developed a working business plan and budget

Secured cost estimates

Begun to arrange the financing

Because of the local or regional nature of most limited partnerships, the investors are typically familiar with the area and can drive by to check on the project. In fact, I recommend that you be wary of offers to invest in a limited partnership in a far-away state. Always ask yourself what local investors might know about the project that makes it unappealing to them. If the deal is good, why does the promoter need to raise money from someone 1,200 miles away?

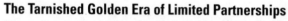

The Tarnished Golden Era of Limited Partnerships

From the late 1960s through 1986, most limited partnerships were designed principally as tax shelters. Brokers sold these partnerships in droves, in part because the deals were laden with heavy sales commissions (frequently 10 percent or more of the amount invested). The promoters of these partnerships took additional fees, which further reduced the amount of the investors' money that could be put to work. Adding insult to injury, the promoters frequently placed themselves ahead of the investors in reaping any benefit of cash flow that came from the deal.

Why did people invest in such a vehicle? There were three reasons:

The stock market was lackluster at that time, and money is always looking for somewhere to go.

Sales organizations aggressively promoted the partnerships in order to reap those large commissions.

The partnerships offered very significant tax sheltering.

The deals were structured so that, by themselves, the tax advantages could make a poor investment attractive to a high-tax-bracket individual. This was very appealing to high earning investors, as during the 1970s the top marginal income tax rate was a very uncomfortable 70 percent. Furthermore, during that period the depreciable life for real estate was a short fifteen-year period and the tax codes permitted the partnerships to accelerate the depreciation and aggressively write off finance costs. The high marginal tax rates, aggressive use of the tax code, and overzealous marketing caused many projects to come to market even though they possessed little economic rationale.

Fortunately, limited partnership abuse came to an end with the passage of the Tax Reform Act of 1986. That act coincided with both an SEC and an IRS crackdown on abusive limited partnerships. Today, the vast majority of limited partnerships are well structured and safe from IRS disqualification.

Structuring a Limited Partnership

In most cases, limited partnerships are locally operated, and investors deal directly with the general partner. Partnership papers can be drawn up any way the partners like. There is no uniform limited partnership formula for fees.

Let's look at a very simple example. (Again, keep in mind that there is no required split and that each partnership will be different. In this example, the general partner has a plan that calls for a $10 million project. He expects to line up 80 percent bank financing, so he is seeking $2 million from investors. He plans to raise that amount from twenty investors, at the rate of $100,000 each.

In the example, each limited partner invests $100,000. We will keep the math uncomplicated and say that this deal has no sales charges, so the full $100,000 goes to the investment. Each investor's $100,000 represents 5 percent of the money in the project ($2,000,000 divided by $100,000 equals 5 percent). However, the partnership documents call for each investor to receive only 4 percent of the package for their investment (4 percent × 20 = 80 percent for the investors). The remaining 20 percent is retained by the general partner in exchange for doing the following:

Accepting the unlimited liability

Locating the site or project

Securing the site

Analyzing the local regulations and restrictions

Developing a working business plan and budget

Securing cost estimates

Arranging the financing

Managing the project to completion

Weighing the Advantages and Disadvantages

In the previous example, the general partner earned 20 percent of the profit with no money invested. The 20 percent was the general partner's compensation for his work, knowledge, and the risk of unlimited liability. The following are the advantages for the limited partners:

- Participation in the real estate market without a personal investment of time

- Limited risk, because of the limited partnership structure

- Opportunity to partner with a professional

Limited partners face some disadvantages as well:

- There is a complete loss of control, as the limited partner can make no management decisions

- The aftermarket for limited partnership units is very small; once invested, you likely must ride it out to the end.

- The project ends when the general partner decides that it should end. (I once invested as a limited partner in a residential apartment complex with a general partner who said he expected to sell the project in seven years and cash out the partners; that partnership is now in its twenty-third year.)

In the example, the general partner took 20 percent of the deal, but I have seen both higher and lower fee structures. It is common for a general partner to take additional fees, such as a construction management fee and/or a property management. Remember that general partners are promoting the deal to make money. As the investor, you must carefully read the offering document to determine if the fees and cost burden are reasonable.

"What if I think the fees are too high? Can I bargain with the general partner to get a better deal?" asks Lou.

"Sure, you could negotiate. But I wouldn't," I reply. "There are so many deals out there, I would simply walk away from this one and seek one that is structured more to your liking."

Real Estate Investment Trusts (REITs)

Real estate investment trusts (REITs) date back to sixteenth-century England. The modern REIT is a creature of the tax code and began in earnest in the early 1960s.

Prior to 1960, REITs were generally private family affairs. Maybe Dad had accumulated a few properties. As he grew older, wise old Dad decided that his children were a bunch of dim-witted fools who could not be trusted to responsibly manage his valuable assets. So he placed his two office buildings and one apartment building in a ninety-nine-year trust for his kids. (That'll show them who's boss.) After Dad passed away, the management of the buildings reverted to the trustee, who just happened to be the law firm that had assisted Dad in setting up the trust. The kids hate this setup, but the law firm loves it because it provides the law firm with a ninety-nine-year stream of income.

Unknowingly, I once rented office space in a building that was in a 100-year trust for the children and grandchildren of the original owner. About twenty years into the trust, the heirs had had enough of the law firm skimming charges and fees off the top of what they saw as *their* inheritance. The heirs sued to break up the trust. The law firm that was managing the trust defended its right to be the building manager and to collect the ongoing management fees for its services. The law firm even charged the trust the cost of its own legal defense. The legal fees left nothing in the trust for building maintenance. Soon building maintenance stopped. I, and many of the other tenants, moved out as our leases expired. I lost track of what happened to that case, but I will bet that the heirs ended up with little after the matter was settled.

Fortunately, public REITs that were formed after 1960 have a very different character from the trust I just described. In 1960, the IRS issued a clarification of the tax treatment of REITs. The 1960 clarification states that if the trust distributes at least 90 percent of its income each quarter to its investors, the REIT qualifies for flow-through tax treatment and does not have a second layer of taxation imposed at the corporate level. The 1960 clarification also placed a few restrictions on REITs:

- At least 75 percent of the funds must be invested in real estate, mortgages, or government securities.

- At least 75 percent of the REIT income must come from rents, capital gains on the sale of real property, or mortgage.

- The REIT must have at least 100 investors.

- The five largest shareholders can own no more than one-half of the outstanding shares.

As a result of the 1960 clarifications and restrictions, today's REITs are a clearly defined investment. REITs are actively managed bundles of properties in which buying, selling, renting, remodeling, and exchanging are ongoing activities. A REIT can be found for every subclass of real estate. You can invest in REITs that buy shopping malls of a specific size, while others buy only malls that include a specific type of store, and still others only buy and fix up older or rundown malls. There are residential property REITs, office-building REITs, hotel REITs—the variations go on and on. The structure of a modern REIT is similar to a mutual fund in that investors' money is placed in a pool, and a manager uses the funds in the pool to make real estate investments.

Selecting a REIT

Investing in a REIT is different from investing in a traditional company. You might decide to make an investment in Merck or Pfizer because you have learned of an exciting drug in their product pipeline. You might invest in Motorola or Nokia because of a cool new phone they are offering. Real estate lacks such revolutionary events. Let's be realistic. Since the invention of indoor plumbing, the high-speed elevator, and air conditioning, not much revolutionary has happened in real estate. So when deciding which REIT to invest in, yield will drive your decision. The rate of yield is the key distinguishing feature of a REIT.

Jack quickly says, "I have seen REIT yields listed in the *Wall Street Journal* and in *Barron's*. I assume that you simply go down the list and select the REIT with the highest yield."

"Not so fast," I respond.

"There are always people of questionable ethics. Because the managers of REITs know that a high yield is the major driver that draws investors to their fund, a few REITs have taken a questionable approach to improving their payout. As I was putting my notes together for tonight, I found five REITs under investigation for paying out more in dividends than they earned from profits. In the short term, the occasional accounting anomaly can result in an exaggerated yield. The REITs under investigation however, have a track record of this activity."

Where do REIT managers get the funds to make these larger-than-income payouts? Some borrow the money and use it to pay dividends, instead of using the borrowed funds to acquire or improve their property. Others use the funds from the sale of new shares to pay dividends. (It seems that Mr. Ponzi's method of doing business is still alive and well.) In any event, such unscrupulous behavior is the exception. Most REITs are ethical and fair businesses.

"So how do you select a REIT?" asks Jack.

"It's a two-step process," I say. "First, you must decide what type of real estate you want to invest in. Second, you select a REIT in that field that offers a good return that is supported by its earnings. This means that not only should you look at the dividend return, you must also check to see that the return is justified by the earnings of the REIT. A dividend that exceeds the earnings may signal a coming disaster."

Understanding the Risks

It may sound as though very little can go wrong for the person investing in a REIT, but (and, here, I suspect you know what's coming) there are some risks to consider:

- Interest-rate spikes: Many REITs are dependent on borrowing that is based on adjustable-rate loans. A spike in interest rates will cause a reduced or even a negative cash flow. The antidote for this is to invest in very conservative REITs that use little leverage.

- A huge inflow of dollars to this investment class: With each additional billion dollars that shows up, the inventory of good properties is further picked over, and the prices of the remaining properties go up to reflect the scarcity. The real challenge for REITs lies ahead as more REITs with more money compete for the same properties.

- Economic downturn in the region or type of property in which the REIT invests: It can happen.

- Industry scandal: People who operate REITS stand to make a lot of money, so we could expect that some of them may be unethical. There are fifty state attorneys general out there, and digging up a REIT scandal would be just the ticket for one of them to make a splash in the press. If the scandal breaks out over a REIT you happen to be invested in, your investment could be slashed to a fraction of its value overnight. As is always the case, review the track record of the REIT and its history of ethical behavior before you invest.

As a note of caution, I suggest you avoid investing in nontraded REITs. The greatest advantage to using a REIT as a real estate investment vehicle is that the shares are widely traded, thus providing the investor with liquidity that is missing from most real estate investments. The nontraded REIT takes away that advantage and so makes for a poor investment.

Diversifying with Limited Partnerships and REITs

If you are actively investing in your own real estate projects, you are most likely to be investing in only one type of property. In that case, investing in REITs can provide investment diversification outside that property type or location. An investment in a REIT or a limited partnership can provide a vehicle for diversifying your investments, without carrying the risk of entering an area of real estate in which you have little interest or experience.

Let's say that you are actively developing and renting office space. You might select a limited partnership or REIT that is invested in senior housing or trailer parks. Such an investment can provide you the safety of diversification without requiring that you become expert in those areas.

17: Becoming a Hands-On Real Estate Investor

All the Profits, All the Work

Anne smiles and proclaims, "This is what I've been waiting for. In spite of the current bad news in the real estate market, I believe that the long-term view is solid. I plan to make the centerpiece of my investments a carefully selected portfolio of properties that I manage myself. I want to be 'hands on.' Besides, what better time to buy than when others are so willing to sell?"

Bob and Jack are both nodding at Anne's logical point of view.

Hands-on real estate investment offers the potential for high returns, but it requires that you understand the risks and techniques involved. As a practical matter, most real estate investors are unlikely to hold more than a few active projects at any one time (unless, of course, their pockets are exceptionally deep). They know that a diversified portfolio is their strongest safety net, and they weaken that net considerably when they concentrate too many assets in any single investment.

Before investing in real estate, consider the following:

- Real estate investments can be lumpy. By that, I mean that real estate investments can require a large lump of your funds. That fact can make it difficult to allocate your investment dollars over several investments.

- Real estate almost always requires the use of financing: the greater the amount of leverage, the greater the risk.

- Active investing in real estate is very time-consuming.

- The liquidity of real estate can be spotty.

Do you remember the 1992 presidential campaign of challenger Bill Clinton versus the incumbent George Bush? The Clinton campaign office supposedly had a large sign that read, "It's the economy, stupid!" What the sign meant was they could talk about anything they wanted, but they always must come back and focus on the topic of the economy.

"I sure do remember that, and it worked, didn't it?" says Jack. "But how does that relate to what we're talking about?"

"Jack," I say, "I am generally reluctant to give investment 'tips,' but at this point I think one is in order."

The number-one element every real estate investor must understand prior to making any real estate investment is this: "It's the exit plan, stupid!"

That's it. I have made several real estate investments, and the secret sauce is knowing and executing your exit plan. It is always about the exit plan. Remember that every month you hold the property you are paying interest, taxes, utilities, and more. The most satisfying real estate deals that I have been in were in-and-out in less than ninety days. Or they were deals that I planned to hold for decades. In the case of the long-term holds the investor can rely on appreciation to make the deal profitable. It is the deals that linger without a clear exit strategy that produce the disappointing internal rate of return for the investor. If a real estate investor does not have a clear exit plan before investing, he or she may be in for a disappointing experience."

Real estate investing can be very profitable, and I am not trying to discourage anyone from entering into this area. However, real estate investing should be approached with an open mind and a heightened level of caution.

Direct Investment in Real Estate

If the fees charged by a limited partnership or REIT turn you off, you will be happy to know that you don't have to pay anyone to do your real estate investing for you. Instead, you can simply do it yourself. (Did I say "simply"?) You won't have anyone to help do the work, but you will be able to keep all the profits.

Here's a to-do list for direct investment:

1. Clarify your concept.

2. Find first-stage funding.

3. Identify the list of professional services you will require.

4. Identify your market area.

5. Search your selected area(s) for the site.

6. Do initial feasibility planning.

7. Do a risk/reward analysis.

8. Write the marketing (sales or leasing) plan.

9. Understand the local codes and restrictions. (Do this early in the process to save yourself time and a lot of frustration later.)

10. Line up funding.

11. Negotiate to secure the land or building.

12. Understand the water, sewer, and electricity services in the community.

13. Hire a professional to conduct an environmental survey and structural inspection. (Don't forget the pest inspection.)

14. Select and establish fees with the project's architect, engineer, general contractor, land planner, surveyor, legal representation, property tax attorney, and so on.

15. Draw a complete set of plans.

16. Obtain permits. (I hate this one.)

17. Complete the design as required by the city building department.

18. Conduct the construction bidding process.

19. Obtain property and liability insurance.

20. Break ground (or rehab) the site.

21. Manage the construction or rehab.

22. Market the project.

23. Complete the construction.

24. Conduct a careful punch-list review (that is, a review of the projects still uncompleted).

25. Carry out the punch-list projects.

26. Lease or sell the property.

27. Pay off all remaining bills and final debts.

28. Set up an escrow account for warranty claims.

Did I mention that being an active real estate investor is time-consuming?

Of course, not every project requires each of the above steps. Before you begin actively investing in real estate, however, be sure that you have allocated ample time so that you are able to complete the project properly.

Choosing Your Approach

The first step on the to-do list is to clarify your concept. Simply put, you need to determine the type of real estate investment you are interested in targeting. Remember, rule one for successful investors is to invest in what you know. By homing in on a single type of real estate investment, you improve your opportunities to become knowledgeable. (Rule Three, "Embrace the Learning Curve.")

Here are just some of the types of real estate you might choose to target:

Undeveloped land	Building single-family residences
Office space	Rehab single-family residences
Retail space	Two- and four-unit apartments (build or rehab)
Strip malls	Five-unit and above residential (build or rehab)
Industrial	Senior housing
Mini warehouses	Trailer parks
City	Suburb
Rural	Build-to-suit

Most investors take a comfort-zone approach when determining the type of real estate in which they want to invest. For example, if you are most at ease investing in shopping malls or warehouse space, you can confine your search to those types of properties. I recommend this approach. You will be investing within your comfort zone and building a set of experiences and knowledge with each passing project that will help improve your results in future projects.

Some brave investors, however, use a return on investment (ROI) approach. The ROI approach takes into account that at any given time, one sector of the real estate market will be offering superior returns to another. ROI real estate investors vary the types of real estate in which they invest, aiming for the sector that offers the highest returns. This approach requires a good deal more knowledge of real estate markets and is not for the newbie.

Identifying Your Professional Team

Don't sell this point short. The professionals you choose to work with are critical to the successful outcome of your real estate investments. A slow architect, a sloppy attorney, or a novice engineer with no connections at your local city building department will cause delays and cost money. In addition to these professionals, you also need to find a good real estate agent, private building inspector, contractor, appraiser, banker, accountant, and (maybe) property manager. Assembling a good team requires time; it will take at least three to five deals for you to fully identify the team of professionals you want to work with. Building your team of professionals is part of the learning curve process embodied in Rule Three, "Embrace the Learning Curve."

You also need to hire a tax attorney. Many investors wait too long to bring a tax attorney into their real estate projects. Aside from loan interest and the cost of construction, taxes could be one of your biggest costs in this type of investment. Property taxes, income taxes, transfer taxes, capital gains taxes, and estate taxes will do more to take money out of your pocket than will the electric bill, water bill, or maintenance costs.

If you are going to use the services of a general contractor, plan to interview several before making your selection. Do the background checks, call references, and obtain proof of insurance. Ask your attorney to help you check for violations, liens, and past lawsuits. Be sure in your interviews to ask how much experience each candidate has with your type of project. An experienced *commercial* general contractor may not be the right choice if you are developing a *residential* building. Another important question is: How much experience does the contractor have working in the city where the project will be located? This is important because each city has its own building code requirements.

If the contractor says any of the following during your interview—and believe me, I have heard each of these—it is time to finish your coffee, close your briefcase, and walk away:

- "I've never worked on this type of project before but, they're all alike."

- "I've never worked in this city before, but they're all the same."

- "Permits? You don't need permits!"

- "Don't waste your money on a set of architectural plans."

- "Trust me, I'm honest."

Here are some final pieces of advice for successfully working with a general contractor:

1. Review the contract with your attorney before signing it. (Excellent boilerplate contracts are available; probably the best are published by the American Institute of Architects.)

2. Demand frequent billings; you don't want any surprises at the end.

3. Demand that the billing statements be sent to you with complete supporting documents.

4. Inspect the site often to be sure that work is proceeding on the promised schedule.

Working with Real Estate Agents

A real estate agent can be a valuable asset when you are seeking an investment property. Because there are well over a million agents in America to choose from, you can be picky. As when choosing a partner, look for an agent whose skills complement your own.

It is generally a good idea to look for an agent who specializes in the locale or the type of property that fits your profile. You should have no difficulty finding agents who specialize in a community, but it might take a bit more work to find an agent who specializes in a specific type of investment property. Working with a knowledgeable agent can dramatically improve the effectiveness of your search. Seek out an agent who has worked in the area ten or more years. She'll know who owns what and, just as important, she is likely to know their real motivations for selling. If you know the neighborhood, but you have weak links to financing, you want to find an agent with strong financing connections.

Frequently, I hear real estate investors say, "I tried working with agents, but they just drove me around and never showed me what I really wanted." My reaction to this is, "That's partially your fault." The first rule when working with any professional is to be clear. Before you start, know what you are looking for. The more specific you can be with the agent, the better for both of you. Here are some of the criteria you need to specify:

- Type of building

- Type of neighborhood, along with a few specific examples

- Clear price range

- Minimum potential rent roll

- Your willingness to consider properties that require improvements

I suggest that you take the time to write out your criteria. This may sound like a silly step, but it can save you hundreds of hours. It will help your agent do his or her job, and it will keep you from looking at properties that you know you are not going to buy. Armed with a clear set of parameters to help narrow the hunt, most agents will be willing to work hard on your search.

You've Got to Kiss a Lot of Frogs: Selecting a Site

One of the differences between a real estate professional and a real estate novice is the time and attention given to the property selection process. A neophyte assumes that the money is made when you sell your real estate investment. The experienced investor knows that the money is made at the time you buy the investment. The investors who do best strive to buy their properties at slightly below market value, an accomplishment that requires knowledge of the market and some hard work. Take your time when looking for your real estate investment property. Remember that if you overpay for an investment property, you will be underwater before you even begin.

Decide before you begin your search whether you are seeking a suburb or city, a depressed neighborhood or one that is up-and-coming, a blue-collar or a premium address. When you buy a property, you really are buying a neighborhood, so learn all you can about the income levels, vacancy rates, educational levels, school systems, and other demographics of the area where you are considering making an investment. Try to look ahead to determine what future competition you might face in your area. Check on the availability of nearby land for construction of competing property types, and pay a visit to the local building department to find out what construction permits are pending in the area.

There are excellent and honest profits to be made in any neighborhood. However, only a few will be suited to your investment style. Making these determinations early will greatly narrow and simplify your property search.

I suggest that you look at *lots* of properties before you buy. The worst thing that can happen is that you find two or three different opportunities that meet your investment profile. That's great; in fact, it will make you a better negotiator. If one seller is a pain in the neck, you can just close your notepad and move on to talk to the next.

$ Making the Offer: Poker, Anyone?

Be ready—you may need to play a little real estate poker. Sellers may tell you that they are "already considering a few other offers that have come in" and that some of those offers look "very interesting." Maybe there are other offers and maybe not—you may never know. The one thing you *do* know is that the seller has just run a ploy that may make you offer more than you would like. *Don't do it.* Stick to your price.

I suggest trying to beat the seller to the punch. When you hand the seller your offer, say something like, "I really shouldn't be making an offer at all. I have an offer out on another property already, and I cannot do both deals." Let the seller figure out if you are bluffing.

Putting It in Writing

Writing an offer is especially important for the person on the weak side of a real estate deal. You are on the weak side if you are the buyer in a seller's market or the seller in a buyer's market. If you are on the weak side, as soon as you are able to bring the other party to a point where you believe a deal is possible, you want to commit the basic facts in writing. (Your real estate agent or real estate attorney is valuable here.)

Don't worry. Offer forms are written with many contingency clauses that can provide multiple doors out of the deal if you later want to back away from a project. Even so, getting the facts committed to paper will add a formal air to the process that encourages both parties to move forward in a professional manner.

Guidelines to Negotiating a Good Deal

The first guideline is to know yourself. If you have a short fuse, a fast temper, or a sarcastic streak, let someone else negotiate the deal. If you ask your lawyer to be your negotiator, expect her to take an adversarial approach. Many sellers do not react well to this approach, so lawyers blow a lot of deals that could have been finalized. Some real estate agents, on the other hand, may be willing to give in on too many points in the negotiations. If you ask a real estate agent to negotiate the deal, be sure that your agent understands your limits.

If you plan to do your own negotiation, here are the simple rules to follow:

1. Be armed with knowledge about the community; the condition of the building; and the cost to fix, repair, and improve it. Know the area rent rates and occupancy rates. The more you know, the better.

2. Say nice things about the seller's building. "Your building is very handsome. You have done a beautiful job, and I'd love to pay what you are asking, but I can't because of . . ."

    . . . the darned economy.

    . . . the darned low rents in this area.

    . . . the darned poor parking around here.

    Remember, the reason that you give the seller as to why you need to pay less for his property should be because of something outside the control of you or the seller.

3. Listen to the seller's stories. He may eventually tell you the real reason why he is selling. You may be able to make a lower offer if you can solve his real problem.

4. Have your financing in place.

5. Be ready to act. The seller is ready to sell now. If you make a contingent offer, most sellers will keep looking for another buyer.

6. Never rely on oral concessions or warrantees. "All valid agreements must be in writing."

7. Stay unemotional and objective. Remember, at its core, this is a simple buying decision.

8. And most of all, relax. This isn't the last opportunity you will find; instead, it's only one property of the millions that are out there.

Checking the Numbers and Income Ratios

To help you make a clear decision as to if you should invest in a specific real estate deal it's a good idea to "run the numbers." You want to review the financial ratios on the project to be sure the purchase meets your investment criteria. Most agents who specialize in income-producing properties will have these ratios ready for you in advance, if your agent does not have them, here is a list of ratios and how to compute the numbers for yourself:

1. Net operating income: (Gross income minus operating expenses)

2. Cash on cash return: (Net operating income minus debt service, divided by cash invested)

3. Total return on investment: (Net operating income minus debt service plus debt reduction, divided by cash investment)

4. Capitalization ratio: (Net operating income divided by sale price)

5. Debt service ratio: (Net operating income divided by debt service)

6. Operating efficiency: (Operating costs divided by total square feet)

7. Break-even ratio: (Total operating costs plus total debt service, divided by gross income)

Many investors like to review additional ratios, such as operating ratio and gross rent multiplier. Again, your agent should be able to compute these numbers for you.

These ratios are helpful because they help you to take a realistic look at the financial picture presented by the investment. Ratios are also helpful when comparing similar investment opportunities to each other. Before leaving this topic, let's take a closer look at a few of the most important ratios you should consider when sizing up the investment potential of a real estate purchase.

The Real Way to Calculate Your Cap Rate

The capitalization, or cap, rate of a real estate investment property is used to determine the estimated value of a property based on a single year of income from the property. When you're running the numbers on investment property, the cap rate is the most quoted and most misleading of all the ratios. The cap rate formula in the preceding list (net operating income divided by sale price) is a shortcut used by almost every real estate agent when describing a property. The difficulty with the number is that it is almost always wrong.

What is wrong with it? It's not *your* cap rate, and that's because one of the components used in the equation is misleading. Remember that to determine this rate you need to know the net operating income, or NOI (total income minus operating costs). Typically the revenue portion of the equation is straightforward. Assuming that you have a current and accurate rent roll, you can easily add the numbers to obtain the property's estimated revenue for one year.

The expense side of the equation is where the difficulty usually lies. Each person manages property differently. Consequently, to determine your true cap rate, you need to recalculate the expense statement that the seller provided. Your accounting treatment and the accounting treatment used by the seller may differ on small items such as auto expense, office expense, and meeting travel charged to the project. You may also differ on bigger issues, such as how management fees are charged. It seems that self-managers forget to value their time and do not pay themselves enough. What about professional fees? If the current owner is an attorney, for instance, he may not be charging the property for legal services.

Next, you need to review the maintenance costs. These costs are frequently scaled back as the seller may have has stopped maintaining the property or, in some cases, failed to charge the last year's work to the property to artificially inflate the NOI.

Only after you have a complete line-by-line recasting of the income statement will you be able to compute your NOI for the project.

Most people divide the NOI by the sale price, but that price isn't the true cost of the property. You may need to add other costs to the sale price, including legal fees, inspection costs, loan application fees, closing costs, tax stamps, insurance binders, and other costs associated with the purchase of the property. Only after you have estimated and added all these costs can you compute the true cap rate.

Don't be fooled by references to a "community cap rate." A real estate agent might warn, "You'd better jump on this one—it's priced at a 9.9 percent cap rate, and everything else in the area is priced at a 7.5 percent cap rate." Hold on: We just said that you manage your property differently from others. Not only is your management style unique, so is everyone else's. That means a community cap rate is a bogus concept.

Know the Most You Should Ever Pay

A critical question that real estate investors must answer is, "What is the maximum amount I can pay for an investment property and still achieve my desired return on investment?" Before your negotiation with the seller, you must know where you draw the line on price. Once you determine the maximum that you can pay, keep the number to yourself. Never share it, just in case the seller is willing to sell for less.

To determine the most you can pay for income property, you will need three pieces of data:

- The property's projected net operating income (NOI)
- The projected annual debt service ratio
- Your desired return on your investment

Let's use these three pieces of data to calculate the maximum amount we can pay for a hypothetical investment property.

Above we have already calculated NOI, so we are a third of the way done. Remember, that the NOI does not take debt service into account.

For our example, we will assume that we are buying a twelve-unit apartment building with a rental rate of $800 per month and an expected 5 percent vacancy rate (12 units × $800 a month × 12 months a year minus 5 percent equals $109,440 projected annual rental revenue). We also will assume a projected operating cost of $51,000 per year (not counting debt repayment or interest costs). Hence, the NOI is $58,440.

Now, let's establish our annual debt service ratio. You can be sure that your debt service will be unique. Your debt service will depend on your goals, your credit-worthiness, the credit-worthiness of the project, your down payment, your time frame for payoff, your lender, and so on.

In our example, we think that we can buy the property for about $500,000, and we plan to make a down payment of $100,000, leaving $400,000 of debt. We are selecting a twenty-five-year amortization period, and the current interest rate is 7.1 percent. To help with our calculation, we can use one of the many mortgage amortization programs available for free on the Internet. Using one of those calculators, we find that the annual debt service cost will be $34,234. We divide that cost by our outstanding balance to determine the debt service ratio: $34,234 divided by $400,000 equals 8.558 percent.

Lastly, we plug in to the equation the rate of return that we want to earn on our investment dollars. In this example, we want to earn a 14 percent return on our investment. We further assume that the property will appreciate at a rate of 6 percent per year. Hence, we will need to earn only about 8 percent a year from operations to realize our 14 percent return on investment goal.

What is the most we can pay and still reach our goal? The formula is simple. Because we are making a 20 percent down payment and we want to earn 8 percent on operations, our calculation looks like this:

$0.20 \times 0.08 = 0.016$, or 1.6 percent.

Now, let put all this together. We need 8.558 percent (to cover the debt) plus 1.6 percent (to satisfy our return requirements); that equals 10.158 percent. So 10.158 percent is the total return we are seeking from our investment property.

Armed with this number, we refer back to the projected net operating income above of $58,440 and divide that number by 10.158 percent ($58,440 / .10158) $575,310.

That's it. We can pay up to $575,310 for this building and still achieve our goals. If the seller will accept $575,310 or less, eureka! If not, we will just smile and move on.

"Stop, stop!" says Bob. "I want to catch up with my notes. I've never heard this formula before, and it can be a real key when selecting a property. I think I've got it, but I want to have my notes in order because this is something I want to be able to refer back to in the future."

A Final Word

As I mentioned at the beginning of this chapter, active real estate investment isn't for everyone. It will consume a great deal of time, energy, attention—and money. If, after reading this overview of some of the responsibilities and risks involved in this type of investment, you remain interested in pursuing real estate, here is the final piece of advice.

Start small.

Be prepared to work your way through the learning curve (Rule Three) and expect that you may waste some time and a few dollars along the way. Active real estate investment has the potential to offer great rewards, but it does require your full attention to earn them.

"Of course, after you purchase your property, you face the next challenge; maintaining your investment. We will take that step after we freshen up our drinks. Tim, are there any cashews left in that bowl near you?" I ask.

18: Managing Your Real Estate Investment

Manage Your Property, or It Will Manage You

There are two ways to profit from most real estate investments. You can buy and hold the property to earn rental income, or you can buy, improve, and sell the property.

If you are a buy, improve, and sell investor, you face the question of just how much you can invest in the enhancement of your property and still hope to earn a profit at resale. All new real estate investors wring their hands over this issue. (If they don't, they should.) The question is difficult because there is no exact formula for finding a right answer. Housing markets fluctuate, neighborhoods change, and unforeseen events unfold. Any of these changes can affect the sale value of an investment property. While you can't control the future, you can attempt to follow a set of guidelines when improving and maintaining your properties so you have the best possible chance of earning a positive return when you sell.

Adding Value Without Diminishing Your Returns

In an ideal world, you could find a way to buy a steady stream of properties significantly below market, then quickly sell them at market price. However, finding such a stream of properties is difficult at best. As a practical matter, if you are buying property with the intention of making a short-term resale at a profit, you will need to add value. But how do you add that value, and how much should you add? As we said earlier, there is no perfect answer to these questions. But based on your investment goals, you can make some assumptions.

If you plan to rent your investment property, you first need to set your rate of return goal. Let's say your rate of return goal from rental income is 8 percent. To achieve that rate, for every $1,000 you invest in improvements, you must be able to increase the rent (above its current rate) by $6.67 a month. ($1,000 × 8 percent equals $80; divided by 12 months equals $6.67 a month.) If you are seeking a 6 percent rate of return from rent, then every $1,000 spent on improvements will require a $5-per-month increase in rental income.

This formula is a nice guideline, but in real life, it can be an uneven method of analysis. For example, my partner and I bought a fourteen-unit building. The previous owner had the rents up as high as the area could warrant. At the time of the purchase, the building had ten occupied and four unoccupied units. We put $6,000 into improving the curb appeal of the building. (We added landscaping, covered the front entrance with a small roof, and built a low wall leading up to the entrance.) After the improvements, the phone began to ring, and we slowly filled the building to 100 percent occupancy. The rate of rent per unit was the same as when we bought the property. However, we now had a fully occupied building. Even though we could not increase the rent, we did improve the rental income by $3,600 a month. (That works out to a 720 percent annual return on our investment in improvements.) In other words, you have to fully consider your property's potential for increased earnings from each possible angle when deciding what improvements you can afford to make.

You also should take into account the potential intangible benefits that might result from adding value to your property. Again using the same example, my partner and I also realized intangible benefits. The improved appearance of the building helped us to attract better tenants. Thus, rent collection problems decreased, and the atmosphere in the building improved. The new tenants took pride in their homes and treated our property more carefully and respectfully.

When considering how to add value to a property you plan to sell, you again must consider your potential for return on your investment. Will a $20,000 kitchen upgrade bring you a $25,000 increase in value at resale time? That depends on your neighborhood and the market conditions at your time of sale. In one neighborhood, adding a swimming pool will increase the value; in another, a pool will decrease the value. Some neighborhoods are all about the bathroom, so money spent there can double the return. In another neighborhood, your best return could come from improving the curb appeal and landscaping the front yard.

A knowledgeable local real estate agent can help you decide which improvements will pay off in your neighborhood. Information about what is selling or what features are important to renters/buyers will be at the agent's fingertips. Deciding which value-added investment to make in your property will be easier if you have the guidance of an experienced real estate agent in your area.

Managing Your Investment Property

If you plan to hold a property to earn rental income, you also must decide who will manage the property. You can choose to manage the property yourself or hire a professional property management company. We don't need to delve into the nitty-gritty details of property management here. I recommend you visit your local bookstore or check Amazon.com to find one of the many well-written books on this topic.

Even if you plan to manage the property yourself, I suggest that you contact one or two professional management companies to get a quote and a description of what services they offer. I find that my interviews with management companies always provide me with useful information. Even if you never hire a property manager, the meeting can be a valuable learning experience. Professional property management is costly, yet going the do-it-yourself route can be very time-consuming.

Some management companies claim that by using their services, you actually lower your costs of ownership. However, I've never known that to be the case in real life. As a practical matter, the amount of time you have available for managing your property will be the deciding factor that will help you determine if you will do the management task yourself or hire a professional management company.

If you decide to use a management company, here are some guidelines:

- Make sure the agreement allows you to fire the management company on very short notice.

- Get a written list of the services the management company will provide.

- Review in detail each report you receive from the management company every month.

- Know the name and contact information for the management company employee who has responsibility for your property. And know how to get a hold of that person at any time.

- Do not sign an agreement that obligates you to use the management company's real estate agency if you decide to sell your property.

Taking Charge of Tenant Leases

Most communities have a standard lease form, but you don't have to use it. Your building is unique, your tenants are unique, and you are unique. What are the things you really care about in your building? Consider that question, and then write a lease that emphasizes those things that matter most to you. Are you concerned with noise levels? Then your lease should say so and have penalties for violations. Are you concerned with too many guests at parties? What about pets, property damage, or the type of vehicle allowed to park in your lot? Ask your attorney to craft a lease that reflects your desires.

Don't feel compelled to stick with some community standard on lease period, either. Believe it or not, I prefer a month-to-month lease. No matter how careful you are when screening new tenants, occasionally you are going to end up with a dud—someone you really want out of your building. If you have month-to-month leases, the end of the lease term is never more than a few weeks away.

I know what you're saying: "With a month-to-month, the tenant could simply leave any time she feels like it and not pay the remainder of her rent." I've got news for you—it's going to happen anyway. Do you really plan to chase the tenant to another city, state, or even another country to collect your rent?

Selling Your Property

Are you ready to sell the property? If so, be sure the property is ready to be sold. Let's begin by assuming that you have maintained your property well. Ongoing maintenance is good practice in any case, and it offers an especially nice bonus at sale time because you won't have to explain away any major defects. Even so, a bit of cosmetic improvement is generally in order before you put a property on the market. I cannot tell you how many buildings I have looked at where owners have let their properties go to seed, with peeling paint, stained and faded wallpaper, unkempt hallways, and so on. You should plan to go to market with the building's mechanicals and cosmetics in good condition. If you do, you can expect to sell it at full value. Poorly maintained buildings, however, are likely to trigger offers that are 15 percent, 20 percent, or even 30 percent below market.

What else can you do to help boost sale price? Depending on your cap rate (described in Chapter 17), you may have a number of options for improving your property and at the same time boosting its sale value. A change to energy-efficient lighting in the common areas to save $2,500 a year on your electric bill can translate into $15,000 to $20,000 extra in the selling price. You should also review your insurance coverage and consider moving to a higher deductible in your final year of building ownership. This may save you $5,000 or more in premium cost, which could translate to $30,000 to $40,000 in the selling price. Increasing the rent by $5 a month per unit on twenty-five units and another $5 a month on twenty-five parking spaces can equal $30,000 more at sale time.

Should you use an agent to sell your investment property? The answer to that question is based on your personal situation. I know that employing an agent is costly; on a large project, it is very costly. If your situation is like mine, however, you might be involved in several projects at any one time (and not all of them in real estate). Advertising and showing a building is a time-intensive process. If you are unavailable for showings, you can really slow down the sale process. If you have loads of time on your hands and some basic sales skills, the cost savings derived from a do-it-yourself approach might be your best alternative. For the rest of us, it's pay-the-commission time.

Gaining the Tax Advantages of a Real Estate Investment

At this point, you may be ready for some good news, and I have some. Real estate investing can generate tax advantages on two levels. The first of these advantages comes to you through depreciation of real property. If you buy income property, you can write it off (depreciate). Residential rental property may be depreciated over twenty-seven and a half years, and most nonresidential real property can be depreciated over a thirty-nine-year period. (See IRS Publication 946, available online at www.irs.gov, for more information.)

The next tax advantage comes from IRS Code Section 1031, which permits a real estate investor to "exchange" his property for a "like kind replacement property." By complying with the IRS rule on this topic, a sale of one property and the purchase of a "like" property are treated as an exchange, thus creating no capital gain from the sale. There are several stipulations, all of which are clearly spelled out by the IRS. The exchange must be for like property—for example, investment property for investment property. "Flipped" houses, condo conversions, and quick-turn rehabs don't qualify for Section 1031, as the IRS considers them businesses, not investments. Here are some other properties that don't qualify under Section 1031:

- Personal residences
- Land under development
- Corporate common stock
- Bonds
- Partnership interests

The room is silent. Bob is quickly writing notes on his pad. He is clearly much more focused on the idea of buying and fixing up that shopping mall he talked about the first time we met. His notes echo our discussion about how to negotiate with the seller and how to compute how much he can spend on improvements. Anne, who also wanted to start a real estate portfolio, is deep in thought. On Mark's pad is the sentence, "Look up REITs."

Each person around the room is thinking through ways to reposition the money they already have so it successfully grows for their future.

After a short pause, I suggest an idea. "It's September. Let's all agree to get together in the city on the last weekend in March. That will give us six months to start to use our new investment techniques. By then, each of us will have information we can share with the others. I'm sure that we will all be interested to hear what the others are accomplishing.

Hearing what everyone is doing will be a good learning experience for all of us."

"That's a good idea but why wait so long?" says Lou. "Does everyone know Mario's restaurant on Canal Street?" Everyone nods in the affirmative. "Good, let's meet there for dinner the last Friday in November. I'll call Mario, he has a small back room I'm sure he'll let us use."

"Then it's set. Mario's in November," says Mark.

Conclusion

And with that began a long tradition of meeting for dinner and discussion once every two months. Each dinner brought another good idea or new investment lesson. The nine rules always held up, no matter the market conditions. Today, five years later, we are still meeting. We threw a party for Mario when he closed his restaurant and moved to Florida last year. Since then we found a new place, and the meetings roll on.

Mark is still in charge of making sure we are organized. Bob is still getting ready to start Weight Watcher's. Above all, we are all better investors.

It is our financial future. We can either leave the future to chance and hope for a lucky break, or we can take charge of our investments and manage our own success. The message of this book is straightforward: We cannot save enough to overcome a poor return. And there are countless opportunities for every investor to achieve excellent high-quality returns with the dollars he or she already has.

Realizing superior returns requires only two things:

1. The desire to achieve them

2. A little knowledge

Save Smart, Earn More contains more than enough information to get anyone started. The desire to achieve greater profits must come from you.

In this book, we have touched on the proven basics for successful investing in the stock market, the options market, fixed investments, buying a business or franchise, and real estate. This information, coupled with the Nine Rules of Successful Investing, can be your ticket to a first-class future for yourself and your family.

The Nine Rules of Successful Investing

1. Invest in what you know.

2. Invest, succeed, repeat.

3. Embrace the learning curve.

4. Avoid losing money.

5. Create a complementary combination of investments.

6. Take charge of one investment.

7. Keep it simple.

8. Trust your method.

9. Rebalance your portfolio.

Appendix A: Helping the Children and Grandchildren with College Costs

America's competitive position depends on the education of today's youth. College education holds many benefits for the nation, with the direct benefits going to those who earn the degrees. According to the U.S. Census Bureau, workers in 2005 who held a bachelor's degree earned an average salary 86 percent higher than the average salary of those with only a high school diploma. Given the very real benefits of a college degree, the cost of attaining a diploma is a wise investment.

Unfortunately, a college education now carries a price tag that is becoming ever more difficult for the typical American family to afford. College costs are rising at a rate of three to four times faster than the rate of inflation. In order to afford the cost burden, families need to start to prepare early.

The federal government has made an effort to give families some relief. Government subsidies for students, in the form of student aid, grants and loans, total almost $100 billion per year. The government also offers tax breaks to those who are saving to pay college costs, and I encourage every family take advantage of these tax-savings opportunity. Here, we focus on two tax-advantaged plans: qualified tuition programs, commonly called section 529 plans, and allowable withdrawals from your IRA plan that can be used to pay education-related expenses.

Just How Much Will College Cost?

Little Carter is only seven years old, and his parents have no way of knowing if he will go to a local city college or choose to be a Yale man. Nevertheless, they need to try to guess how much money the little darling will require in the course of earning his college degree. If you have children or grandchildren, you are faced with the same guessing game.

If your heart is set on sending your child or grandchild to a private university, hold on to your hat. In 2007, tuition at the nation's private universities averaged $35,000. (I guess it's expensive to maintain ivy.) Even if college cost inflation drops to 5 percent per year, in ten years, little Carter's freshman year at a private school will cost almost $50,000. A full four-year degree could easily reach $200,000.

Public universities are less pricey, but they aren't cheap. The University of Michigan undergrad school tuition for the 2007 academic year was $10,100 for an in-state student, and $31,400 for out-of-state tuition. Of course, the University of Michigan is one of the more expensive state-run schools. The 2007 tuition at the University of Maryland was about $7,500 per year for in-state students, and universities in California were downright bargains at $2,550 to $3,000 a year.

The cost of tuition is only one of the expenses that college students incur. Books, supplies, room and board, travel, maybe a car, clothes, and walk-around money should all be included when you make your cost estimate. College Web sites offer a good estimate of the total costs you might expect. Look for a section on the Web site titled "Budget" or "Total cost of attendance."

Tapping Your IRA

For the most part, IRAs are retirement planning vehicles, but the IRS has become more liberal when viewing IRAs as a resource to fund interim capital needs. The IRS now permits people to withdraw funds from their IRA prior to age fifty-nine and a half without a tax penalty if the withdrawals are made within very clearly defined limits. The costs of higher education are among the expenses for which the IRS allows for penalty-free withdrawals. (You still pay regular income tax on withdrawals.)

The rules that permit withdrawals from an IRA to pay for higher education costs are relatively liberal and straightforward:

- The education can be for you or for a family member.

- The education must be provided by a qualified higher-education institution.

- The amount withdrawn may not exceed the actual out-of-pocket costs for the education.

For example, if your little Sammy's tuition and other qualified expenses are $21,000 for the year, and Sammy receives grants and scholarships totaling $6,000, the amount that may be withdrawn penalty-free is limited to $15,000 ($21,000 minus $6,000).

An early IRA withdrawal may help you pay college costs, but it creates another problem. This money was to have been your retirement savings. Funds withdrawn from an IRA cannot be made up in later years and hence will not be available at retirement as you planned.

If you find that money is tight as you prepare to pay college expenses, you may choose to reduce your contribution to your retirement savings plans and set that money aside for college. If you find that you must cut back on your retirement savings to fund a college savings plan, do so with a paring knife, not with an ax. Long-term compounding of retirement saving is so significant that $1,000 saved for your retirement today will have a greater impact on your retirement than $10,000 invested twenty-five years from today. Consequently, I suggest that for the purpose of saving for college costs, most families should consider starting a 529 plan before contemplating a withdrawal from their IRA.

529 Savings Plans

For many years, wealthy families have set up prepaid tuition agreements with their favorite colleges, but the use of such plans by average Americans is relatively new. Government-sanctioned college savings plans began at the state rather than federal level. The states of Michigan, Florida, and Wyoming were the first to offer organized college savings plans in the mid-1980s. In these early plans, a family could deposit money directly with the state. The state placed the money in a separate account, which it invested, with the goal that the growth of the investment would equal or outpace the rising cost of college tuition. When the child was ready to attend college, the state would make a direct payment from the separate account to a college on its approved list.

Then, the IRS (a real party-pooper if there ever was one) dropped a fly in the ointment by declaring that any earnings of the separate account were taxable in the year earned. In addition, the IRS ruled that the separate account was a trust and thus taxable at the trust tax rate. The states spent much of the next ten years in and out of tax court. The IRS won some rounds; the states won others.

In 1996 (an election year), Congress was anxious to show how much it cared about the needs of American families. So, it tucked into the Small Business Job Protection Act of 1996 a provision to help families pay for college costs. The provision, called Qualified Tuition Programs (QTP), is today better known by its section number, 529. This small section of a much larger bill gave form and sanction to the old concept of setting aside money to be used later for educational expenses.

Today, 529 plans are the single best vehicle for saving for education costs. The plans are still relatively new and evolving. If history is a guide, we can expect that 529 plans will continue to become more flexible and family friendly.

An important thing to remember is that 529 plans aren't just for kids. If you plan to return to college in the future, you can set up a 529 naming yourself the beneficiary. (See you in study hall!)

The 411 on 529 Plans

A 529 plan is a tax-preferred savings plan designed to help families pay for future education expenses. These plans are offered only by states (or state agencies) or by eligible educational institutions. As such, the rules vary slightly from state to state. Most 529s are funded by making an investment in a mutual fund. The mutual fund shares are then held inside the 529 plan.

Colleges saving accounts fall into two categories: prepaid tuition plans and savings plans. A prepaid plan offers you the opportunity to prepay tuition costs at a state-run college or university, thereby protecting yourself from tuition increases that might come between the time that you make your payment and the time the beneficiary is ready to attend. Early prepaid plans covered only tuition costs.

The 1996 Small Business Job Protection Act made the 529 plan an appealing alternative to the more restrictive prepaid tuition plans. Instead of prepaid tuition programs, these are savings plans that allow you to pay for a variety of higher-education services. Some of the elements of 529 plans will remind you of the rules for a Roth IRA:

1. There is no federal income tax deduction for money contributed to a 529 plan, so contributions are made with after-tax dollars.

2. Once contributed to a 529 plan, investments grow tax-free.

3. Withdrawals from 529 plans are not taxed as along as they are used to pay qualified higher education expenses.

Like any tax-preferred plan, 529 plans come with a long list of regulations and restrictions, but that should not discourage you from considering this savings vehicle. The rules governing 529 plans are logical and, in many cases, downright liberal.

Qualified Expenses

As far as tuition goes, funds from 529 savings plans may be used to pay the cost of attending any qualified educational institution. IRS Publication 970 (available at *www.irs.gov*) defines this category in detail. It includes virtually all of America's accredited public, nonprofit, and proprietary postsecondary institutions, as well as "certain educational institutions located outside the United States." (If you are unsure if your selected school qualifies, call the school's administration office. They hear this question every day and can give you a complete answer regarding their institution.) In addition to tuition, other qualified expenses include fees, books, required supplies, and reasonable expenses for room and board.

The money inside a 529 plan has some protection. Most states provide protection of 529 assets from claims of creditors. At the federal level, money in a 529 plan is protected from bankruptcy judgments. (For specific questions regarding creditor protection, always seek legal counsel in your state.)

Be realistic in deciding how much to invest in the 529 plan. When setting your savings goal, remember that your 529 plan investment earns money without incurring income tax. This reduces the amount you must contribute to reach your goal.

Designating a Beneficiary

When opening a 529 savings plan account, you must name a living person as your designated beneficiary. (Typically, it is the future student for whom the benefits are intended.) The beneficiary need not be related to you. Although it is rarely necessary, you can change the designated beneficiary in a 529 plan. You can name only one designated beneficiary per plan. If you have three children and want to save for the college costs of all three, you should set up three separate plans. If you are planning for your own second-career education, you can name yourself as the beneficiary.

Contributing to the Plan

529 plans do not have income restrictions as do some retirement savings plans. However, they do have state-imposed total contribution limits. The limits, which vary from state to state, are typically in the $250,000 to $350,000 range. If you feel the need to exceed those limits, you can set up separate plans in another state or states. Of course, you had better be sure that your little genius carries through with your view of the future because there is no upside to having an overfunded 529 plan.

An Overfunded 529 Account

Maybe you were too generous in your contributions, or possibly the mutual fund you bought inside the 529 was wildly profitable or, maybe Junior announces that he already knows everything so he sees no need to go to college. (At a time like this, expect Junior to also tell you that Bill Gates was a college dropout and he seems to have done just fine for himself.)

So here you sit, holding a well-funded 529 plan with no qualified higher-education costs to use it on. There are three options:

1. Simply close the plan and liquidate the contents. In that year, you will pay income tax on the full amount of the earnings of the account, plus a 10 percent tax penalty.

2. Just forget about it for a year or two. Leave the account in place without any additional investment. Who knows? Maybe Junior will change his mind after he gets tired of his minimum-wage job.

3. Change your designated beneficiary. The newly named beneficiary must be a member of your family, and the new beneficiary cannot be a lower generation than the original beneficiary. A violation of either of

these restrictions could cause the originally intended beneficiary or the new recipient to pay gift tax.

In general, contributions to a 529 plan should be limited to the current annual gift exclusion (currently $12,000). The IRS permits you to make up to five years of gifts at once ($60,000), on the assumption that you will not be making other gifts to the same beneficiary during that five-year period. If you plan to take advantage of the five-year gift allowance, you should see your tax professional, who will ask that you complete IRS Form 709.

What happens if more than one person opens a 529 saving plan naming the same beneficiary? A 529 plan beneficiary is allowed to receive benefits from more than one account. However, remember that the total contribution limit is per beneficiary, not per account. If Mom and Grandma both plan to open an account for little Lily, they must communicate with each other and coordinate their savings efforts.

Gifts made to a 529 account are considered to be "complete," meaning that money is out of your estate and is not subject to estate taxation in the event of your death.

Finally, contributions to a 529 must be in the form of cash or a cash equivalent. In other words, you cannot transfer the title to a piece of property that you own to a 529 plan. (Sorry, Charlie, you'll have to sell the property, pay the capital gains tax, then contribute to Junior's 529.)

Taxes on Withdrawals

As with any decision concerning taxes, you should check the information I provide here with a tax professional. Tax rules are always subject to change.

Withdrawals made from a 529 plan that are used to pay qualified higher-education expenses, as defined by the IRS, are tax free.

Investments made in a 529 plan have limited flexibility. Unlike your IRA, where you can make trades with very few restrictions, 529 plans generally restrict the types of investments you can make and how often you can move or reallocate your investment. Typically, money in these plans can be transferred or reallocated only once in a twelve-month period. Moving funds more often will cause the IRS to treat the movement as a withdrawal, thus incurring income tax and the 10 percent penalty.

Using 529 Plan Funds

The time has come.

You have diligently contributed to a 529 plan for your designated beneficiary, and now you are ready to start paying those college expenses. To be sure that you preserve the income-tax-free distribution status of money you withdraw from your 529 savings plan, keep a clear paper trail. The easiest way to do that is to ask your 529 plan custodian to send checks, in the amount you request, directly to the college or university (or even the landlord, when paying housing costs.) That way you never touch the money, and the IRS will be comfortable that the funds were used for qualified education expenses. Not every expense can be paid directly, however. If you pay some of the expenses and you want to be reimbursed from the 529 plan, instruct the custodian to send the check to you. Keep a folder containing receipts for the items for which you are being reimbursed, and be sure that the inflow of money you receive from the custodian does not exceed the outflow paid for qualified education expenses. Any earnings that you receive from the 529 that are in excess of your actual qualified education expense will be taxed at ordinary income tax rate plus a 10 percent penalty.

To help you maintain your records, your 529 plan custodian will send a form 1099-Q to you (and to the IRS) for each year that money is drawn from the plan.

Spacing your withdrawals can be tricky, and your individual circumstances must be your guide. For example, if you are sure that you have adequate funds in the 529 to cover all the qualified education expenses for your beneficiary's full college career, then draw money as the expenses occur, and try to use up all the money in the 529 account.

If, as is the case in most families, your 529 plan will cover only a portion of college expenses, you must decide if you want to draw funds to pay for all qualified expenses until the 529 runs dry or spread the assets over time by using a portion of the funds each year.

If you expect that you will use a combination of "pay as you go" and student aid or grants to cover the costs, you can spread out the drawdown. If, on the other hand, you plan to make up the shortfall by using student loans, you should spend down as much as possible in the early years. This will help your student to qualify for student financing and will also delay the time when interest on the debt starts to accrue.

What if the scholarship gods smile on your family, and your son or daughter gets a full scholarship to the school of his or her dreams? Don't cash out your 529 savings plan immediately. Even the best scholarship might not pay for all qualified expenses associated with your child's education. If you find that you truly do not need the 529 funds for college expenses, you can withdraw funds without a tax penalty up to the amount of the scholarship, or you may consider a rollover. A rollover will allow you (with no income tax cost) to move the funds saved for one child to another qualified designated beneficiary.

Be a Smart Saver

School is expensive. As a practical matter, many families cover college costs using a combination of resources. Some students rely on financial aid, scholarships, grants, and loan programs to supplement savings. And don't forget that your son or daughter can work to help cover a portion of the costs. Lastly, some people consider taking a second mortgage on their home to help pay college costs. Before you take out a second mortgage, I recommend that you explore student loans. Armed with information on both types of financing, you can better compare interest rates, payback requirements, and tax treatment of interest payments.

Appendix B: Your Next Home

For many people, part of retirement planning is answering the question "Where will we live?" Even though this is not an investment topic in the traditional sense, this question is intertwined in almost every element of retirement planning.

Reality Check: Reconciling Your Priorities and Financial Boundaries

Moving to a new home is one of the biggest changes most people make in their adult lives. Given the mobile nature of our culture and economy, more people are moving more often than ever before. Employment relocation is a major trigger for many moves, but there are other equally common reasons people seek a new home:

- Lower cost of living: Several recent studies have concluded that where you choose to live has a greater impact on how long your money will last than how much you have saved for retirement. You may love living in scenic San Francisco or fast-paced Manhattan, but the high cost of living in these and other parts of the country can put a serious dent in lifelong savings. You don't need to retire to a cave in the Badlands of North Dakota, but you can reduce your cost of living by 30 percent to 40 percent if you are willing to give up your view of the lake and the convenience of those five-star restaurants within walking distance of your current digs.

- Lower home-ownership costs: Sure, you needed the big house when it was full of children, but they are grown and on their own. Do you still really use all five bedrooms and four bathrooms? Even if you want ample space when the kids come to visit, it may not make sense to maintain all the extra space for those few family gatherings. The maintenance, utilities, taxes, and other expenses of a large property can require more of your resources as you (and your home) age, and that's typically the stage where you want to spend more time traveling, relaxing, and visiting with family and friends. Your living space should fit the life you have now, not the one you used to have.

- Enough cold weather, already: If you're like me, you contract a guy with a pick-up truck and a snow blade to clear your driveway each time it snows. And if you're like me, you wonder why you get eight bills for snow removal when it only snowed six times. You may also be wondering (as I do) how he manages to shear the heads off almost every sprinkler outlet within fifty feet of where he was supposed to plow.

For these reasons and more, people start to consider their next move as they approach retirement. Although some retirees decide to ditch the responsibilities of home ownership altogether, there are some advantages in investing in a home:

- Control: You can do what you like with your property. If you want to paint the outside bright purple, go right ahead (unless you live in a neighborhood with an association that rules in such matters). Do you want to put a $200,000 kitchen in your $150,000 house? Be my guest.

- Appreciation: Traditionally, houses have appreciated at or slightly above the rate of inflation.

- Tax advantages: Interest paid on a residential mortgage is tax-deductible (if you itemize on your federal income tax return), as are real estate taxes. The deduction is available for up to $1 million of home mortgage debt, for either a primary or secondary home. One of the major advantages to home ownership is the tax deductibility of mortgage interest, even though most of this advantage goes away as you pay down your home loan. Many retirees have equity from the sale of their former residence, and it is common for them to make a large down payment on the new property. This decision reduces their monthly payments, but it also reduces the value of the interest deduction for home ownership.

There are also negatives to home ownership:

- Maintenance: Every house—new, old, and in between—requires maintenance.

- Reduced liquidity: Money tied up in your home is not available for other opportunities. Sure, you can borrow against your home, but you must pay interest to do so.

Many retirees opt for condominium living. This option offers the benefits of private ownership while eliminating most maintenance chores.

How Much Money Will You Need?

Today's homebuyers are lucky when it comes to valuing a property. The Internet puts a lot of current information at your fingertips. You can go online to do everything from shopping for a new home in a new city to visiting a home-value estimator service, such as Zillow.com or ABC's of Real Estate (at *www.realestateabc.com*), to get a rough estimate of the value of almost any home in the United States.

The classic formula for calculating your mortgage capability is actually pretty good. It says that your mortgage payment should be no more than 28 percent of your total income, and that your total debt payment (mortgage plus other monthly debt) should amount to no more than 36 percent of your total income. We talk more about mortgages later, but for now, just remember that you can't rely on a mortgage company to determine just how much mortgage you can afford to carry or how much total cost-of-ownership expenses you can carry. You know your lifestyle and standards, so try to keep *all* of your financial needs in mind when choosing your next home.

If you haven't bought a new home for a few years, you might need a short refresher course regarding the expenses involved in the process. The first thing to keep in mind is that the monthly mortgage payment represents only a portion of the home's ongoing expenses. Depending upon the type of home you purchase (single family, townhouse, or condo), you need to add some or all of these items to your yearly cost of home ownership:

- Insurance: The cost of homeowner's insurance varies according to the location, age, size, and condition of the structure. In 2007, the Insurance Information Institute placed the average premium at an estimated

$868. Remember, that was an estimate of an average premium—yours could be much higher or lower.

- Property taxes: These taxes are a factor of the local tax rate times the value of your home. Go online to obtain information about local property tax rates.

- Utilities: Energy rates vary from location to location. The only way to project utility costs for a new home is by asking for energy cost information on homes of similar size in your new community.

- New appliances and furniture: If you need to replace or add to your furnishings, plan for that expense as you prepare your new move budget. If you are leaving your old appliances behind, remember to include their replacement costs as a move-in necessity.

- Repair and maintenance: These expenses can have a direct impact on the affordability of your home. That historic beauty with the wrap-around porch and original shutters has indisputable charms, but when the time comes to scrape and paint the thing, you may wish you had chosen the brick ranch style down the street. That two-acre yard is a real paradise, but what happens when you no longer want to devote half of your weekend to mowing or when you tire of paying a yard service $100 a week for their assistance? Again, don't let your heart lead your wallet down the wrong financial path.

Pest control, housekeeping, redecorating, landscaping—the costs of home ownership are many and diverse. Keep all of them in mind when considering your next home.

Preparing to Buy

Buying a new home involves a lot of decisions and housekeeping chores required to get your finances in order. If you are planning to buy a new home within the coming year, I recommend that you follow a few simple rules:

- Get preapproval for a mortgage loan. You need to know what lenders think you can afford to pay for a house, even though their limits may be higher than you are willing to borrow. Checking your credit score ahead of time and lining up preapproval for a loan will give you bargaining power in your new home purchase.

- Keep major purchases to a minimum. When you have your credit score and preapproval in place, don't tinker with them by buying a new car or changing jobs, unless you absolutely have to.

- Keep your search focused on realistic limits. Even when you have carefully determined your buying criteria and financial limits, when looking at new properties, "feature creep" quickly leads to "price creep." Do not be lured into spending more money than you can afford by amenities that you do not need.

- Don't become best friends with your realtor or a seller. Find the best real estate agent you can find—interview at least three, ask for references, and check them out—then maintain a good working relationship with the agent. Real estate agents, like sellers, have reason to encourage you to spend more, so be sure that you follow your own guidelines when searching for a new home. As you move into negotiations, you do not want your bargaining power to be compromised by emotional ties. This is a business decision, not a marriage.

- Educate yourself. Learn everything you can about the home, neighborhood, city, state, or even country that you are considering moving to. Walk the street, visit nearby businesses, read local newspapers, and—above all—get thorough property inspections from reputable inspection services. The more you know, the less likely you are to make the wrong move.

Financing Your Nest

Okay, you have found the home of your dreams—congratulations! Now the real work begins, as you go about financing your move. Of course, you can cut down on the amount of hassle inherent in this process with planning and preparation.

Choosing a Loan Type

Few people pay cash for their new homes, given the cost of most properties and the tax advantages of carrying a mortgage. What kind of mortgage loan is best? Today, borrowers have options:

- Fixed-term mortgages: This type of loan used to be the standard. These loans extend over a specified period of time, typically fifteen, twenty, or thirty years, and their interest rate never varies. Fixed-term mortgage loans are good choices when you plan to remain in a property for an extended period of time and you want your monthly payments to be the same today as they will be at the end of the loan term.

- Adjustable rate mortgages (ARMs): These loans typically have a short period of one to three years during which the interest is fixed at a relatively low rate. After that time, the rate (and, therefore, your monthly payments) rise and fall along with changes to the prime-lending interest rate. These loans are popular with those who plan to remain in a home for a short period of time and want to keep their payments as low as possible.

- No-money-down loans: These are still an option. However, following the real estate market downturn of 2006 and 2007, the pitfalls of such loans became painfully evident, and this type of loan is no longer recommended except in very special situations.

Reducing Maintenance

What if you want to stay in your present home but the costs of maintaining the home are too great a burden?

One possibility is to use a reverse mortgage. A reverse mortgage allows you to remain in your present home. It will provide you money based on the equity in your home. Reverse mortgages can make payments to you either in a lump sum or in monthly installments. There is no repayment requirement of this type of loan as long as you live in the house. The loan becomes due only when the borrower dies, sells the home, or permanently moves out of the home.

The exact amount that you can borrow is based on a combination of the amount of equity you have in your home and your age. To qualify for a reverse mortgage, you must be at least sixty-two years of age.

Reverse mortgages can be an excellent solution for many people who want to stay in their home. However, a reverse mortgage is not without costs. In addition to the interest that accrues on the amount you borrow, there will be the costs of a new mortgage. This will include an appraisal fee, termite inspection, a loan origination fee, a mortgage insurance fee in some cases, a monthly servicing fee, and other standard documentation recording or closing costs.

The next cost of a reverse mortgage is the decreasing equity in your home. As the name implies, a reverse mortgage is the opposite of a traditional mortgage. With a traditional mortgage, the equity in your home increases each month as you make payments. With a reverse mortgage, the equity in your home decreases each month as you receive another payment and the interest due accrues. The good news is that because of reverse mortgage insurance, *which you must buy*, your equity can never fall below zero.

The reverse mortgage industry is under the jurisdiction of the U.S. Department of Housing and Urban Development (HUD). If you are considering a reverse mortgage, your first stop should be the HUD Web site (*www.hud.gov/buying/rvrsmort.cfm*) to gather all the information you should know before making a decision.

Finding the Right Lender

How do you go about finding a good lender? Traditional lenders include large banks and credit unions. As nonprofit member-owned agencies, credit unions tend to offer lower interest rates than do large banks. Large banks, however, tend to have more assets available for loans.

No matter which lending route you choose, your search for a lender can begin online. Most lending institutions post current interest rates and other information about their mortgage loan offerings on their Web site. If you don't have the time to do your own comparison shopping, or if your credit is a bit less than spotless, you might benefit from using a mortgage broker. These folks charge a fee, but they will take care of tracking down the best mortgage deal for your circumstances, and they may even negotiate a better rate with some lenders. Your real estate agent might also be able to provide some help in finding a lender. Many realtors have existing relationships with lenders, which can result in better rates for borrowers.

Before you agree to accept a loan offer from any mortgage broker, I suggest that you do a little detective work and comparison-shop the offer. Remember, *you* are the person most concerned with the wisdom of your financial decisions. That means you cannot rely solely on the guidance of others when it comes to making your financial decisions.

Index